Squeezing Good
Out of Bad

JAMES N. WATKINS

Lighthouse Publishing
of the Carolinas
www.lighthousepublishingofthecarolinas.com

SQUEEZING GOOD OUT OF BAD BY JAMES N. WATKINS
Published by Lighthouse Publishing of the Carolinas
2333 Barton Oaks Dr., Raleigh, NC, 27614

978-1-941103-00-5
Copyright © 2014 by James N. Watkins

Available in print from your local bookstore, online, or from the publisher at:
www.lighthousepublishingofthecarolinas.com

For more information on this book and the author visit: www.jameswatkins.com

Brought to you by the creative team at LighthousePublishingoftheCarolinas.com: Eddie Jones, Rowena Kuo, and Meaghan Burnett.

Library of Congress Cataloging-in-Publication Data
Watkins, James.
Squeezing Good Out of Bad / James N. Watkins, 2nd ed.

Printed in the United States of America

Praise for *Squeezing Good Out of Bad*

A book that will make you laugh, think, and start looking at those sour places of life in a whole new way. I really enjoyed reading it.

~ **Martha Bolton**
Writer for Jeff Allen, Bob Hope, Phyllis Diller, Mark Lowry

Jim fills each page with thirst-quenching lemon aid! His humility and insight are all the more compelling because he shares the lemons of heartache in his own life. An uplifting and encouraging read!

~ **Marybeth Hicks**
Columnist for *The Washington Times*

Jim helps us find perspective in those life-puckering situations, find power for coping, and even helps us find purpose in the pucker.

~ **Rhonda Rhea**
Author of *Amusing Grace* and *High Heels in
High Places —Walking Worthy in Way Cute Shoes*

Jim Watkins is clearly a man who knows how to laugh and how to cry . . . and when one will be more effective than the other. Discover this godly wisdom for yourself by enjoying this important book as you make sense of life.

~ **Heather Gemmen**
Author of *Startling Beauty*

Fabulous! Very funny and very clever, but also full of so much wisdom.

~ **Rene Gutteridge**
Best-selling author of *The Ultimate Gift* and *Boo*

Jim's sense of humor always lightens my load. He's just flat out funny. I cannot tell you how encouraging that is.

~ **Steve DeNeff**
~Author of *More Than Forgiveness*

Witty, insightful and downright entertaining! After reading *Squeezing Good Out of Bad*, you'll have a whole new outlook on life.

~ **Tim Bete**
Author of *In The Beginning . . . There Were No Diapers*
and director of the Erma Bombeck Writers' Workshop

My purpose in writing is to encourage you and assure you that the grace of God is with you no matter what happens.
1 Peter 5:12b NLT

Dedication

To my family, who has been a source of encouragement
through life-puckering problems.

Contents

Foreword

Have you ever lost track of a container or two in the deep recesses of your refrigerator? Just today, I found a lemon in the refrigerator door that had *grown legs*. I didn't even touch that one. Once they're past the tadpole stage, I try not to make them angry. Sometime before the lemon started to walk upright, however, I knew I really had no choice but to wage war against the beast and its assorted furry and fuzzy friends.

It's a good thing putrefying foods have a built-in stench alarm to remind us it's time for a fridge cleaning. There are a few of us who choose to ignore the alarm now and then. It's a courageous move. Extremely dangerous, but courageous. I've heard that if left to themselves for too long, leftovers start forming gangs.

Not too long ago, I found a translucent container hiding under some brown lettuce and a bag of stiff tortillas. I peered through the thing and, horror of horrors, found beefy macaroni. Maybe beefy macaroni doesn't usually horrify you. But when you consider the fact that when I put it in there, I'm pretty sure it was just plain old macaroni, you can understand why I hesitated to open the fridge door unarmed after that. I considered a whip and a chair. Can oven spray wound macaroni? I at least tried to keep a sharp stick handy.

Cleaning the fridge is no small job. You can't grab a magazine and pull up a chair to start this kind of cleaning process. No, you have to get serious, don some extra heavy rubber gloves and possibly a "hazmat" suit, stand up, and all but climb in. You have to be strong, stand, and fight.

There are battles in this life that are so much more intense than the fridge gang wars. There are life-puckering problems that threaten to take us to the mat. Sorry, I'm starting to mix metaphors, but how can we find everything we need to be strong?

Praise God, He doesn't send us into battle unprepared. We don't have to worry about muscle. We're reminded in 1 Samuel 17:47 "the battle is the LORD's." That lemon can't take me!

I'm praising God, too, for muscle-building, power-punching books like this one. Jim helps us find perspective in those life-puckering situations, find power for coping, and even helps us find purpose in the pucker. We're getting armed for the fight! Sitting around whining about the sour stuff? No way. We're picking up the whip and the chair. We're standing up and climbing in. We're learning how to be strong, to stand, and to fight!

So go ahead. Let *Squeezing Good Out of Bad* beef you up, spiritually speaking. No, not like the macaroni. We can find pucker power as we learn to stand in the power of the Lord, to squeeze meaning out of those life-puckering situations and become more like "lemon-tamers." Believe it or not, even in the pucker, we can find amazing sweetness.

Now if you'll excuse me, I'm going to take my lemon for a walk. Heel, boy.

Rhonda Rhea
www.rhondarhea.org

Thanks!

A great big bushel of thanks to:

Cynthia Ruchti and Kathy Carlton Willis for their kind but constructive editing of the manuscript

Jeanette Levellie for writing the study questions

The Christian Humor Writers Group for their encouragement that kept me going through a whole fruit stand of lemons.

10

When life gives you lemons don't confuse them with hand grenades
Identify the problem

I have in my right hand, direct from my home office in Corn Borer, Indiana, today's top ten list:

When life gives you lemons . . .

10. Don't confuse them with hand grenades (Identify the problem)

9. Check the delivery slip (Determine if it's your problem)

8. Sell them on eBay (Profit from the problem)

7. Paint smiley faces on them (Laugh at the problem)

6. Join a citrus support group (Share your problem)

5. Use as an all-natural, organic astringent (Grow from the problem)

4. Don't shoot the delivery driver (Forgive the problem-maker)

3. Call in the Master Gardener (Take the problem to a higher level)

2. Grow your own orchard (Live a fruitful life despite—or because of—the problem)

1. Give off a refreshing fragrance (Live a lemon-fresh life)

Life is filled with lemons; those life-puckering, lemon-juice-in-the-eye events we all encounter.

Some are only temporary: intestinal flu, crashed computers, lactose intolerance, sadistic dental hygienists, overdrawn checking accounts, and IRS audits.

Others, however, leave a long-lasting bitter taste: chronic illnesses, family feuds, prodigal children, and death. M. Scott Peck in his best-selling book, *The Road Less Traveled,* writes:

> Life is difficult. This is a great truth, one of the greatest truths. It is a great truth because once we truly see this truth, we transcend it. Once we truly know that life is difficult—once we truly understand and accept it—then life is no longer difficult. Because once it is accepted, the fact that life is difficult no longer matters.

Or to put it more succinctly, Roger Anderson reminds us, "Some days you're the pigeon; some days you're the statue."

For instance, I hate all the problems involved in flying! It's not that I'm afraid to fly; I simply hate the hassles of delayed and/or cancelled flights, lost luggage, ten-dollar hamburgers and two-dollar Diet Cokes, onboard movies with Adam Sandler, and most of all, increased security. Since the 9/11 terrorist attacks, airlines have gone from *Def. Con. Dumb Questions at the Desk* ("Did someone you don't know give you a bomb to carry on your flight?") to *Def. Con. Take Off Your Shoes and Belt.*

So, I've been patted down in India (the security guard seemed to enjoy his work just a little too much). Had my skivvies publicly displayed and thoroughly examined in Portugal and Australia (fortunately, at the time they were in my suitcase!).

But the absolute worst was at the Detroit airport in the U.S. of A.

I dutifully put my watch and belt in the little plastic tub. Took off my jacket, placed my carryon bag on the conveyor belt, had my three-ounce-or-less liquids, creams, and gels in the required one-quart clear plastic bag and went through the metal detector without a single beep.

Suddenly, a burly security guard pinned me against the wall with a firm grip around my throat. (Envision Darth Vader lifting up that poor enlisted man by his throat in "Star Wars.") Security guards and police converged on my carryon bag and began digging through it like stray dogs through an overturned garbage can. The top dog glared at me, paused, and then dramatically pulled out of my carryon bag . . . a hair dryer.

Darth let my feet return to the floor and mumbled, "It looked like a handgun."

Life is like that—deceptive and disturbing.

So, the first thing to do when the lemon truck pulls up to your front door is to carefully examine the delivery slip.

"Sorry, not my problem. You want to deliver that load to The Department of Homeland Security, my ex-spouse, or [fill in the blank]." Don't sign for things that are facts of life and not your problem.

There's another possibility, however. What we may perceive as a lemon—some life-puckering problem—may indeed be the event that produces a sweet, fruitful future for us. And worse, what seems perfectly safe and harmless can blow up in our face!

For instance, I'm thankful for my kidney stone in 1991 (I'm mostly thankful it was in 1991 and not today!) Experiencing the sensation of having a semi tractor-trailer with snow chains and a load of rolled steel park on my lower back puts life into perspective.

So, when my daughter called Lois and me at 1 AM in the middle of winter and said, "Uh, Dad, did you know that a '95 Neon can straddle a traffic island?" I could honestly say, "Hey, sure beats a kidney stone."

It's also worked for the time my mother-in-law backed into our brand-new car. When I forgot to *ever* change the oil in our new car—and needed a whole new $4,127 engine. When I lost a great job as an editor at a publishing house due to corporate down-sizing. When we were spending half our vacation time sitting in a traffic jam in downtown Chicago with a stick shift, in August with no air-conditioning, and two kids in the back seat waging a fight to the death. I could confidently say, "Hey, sure beats a kidney stone."

Unfortunately, some lemons are worse than a kidney stone. I've experienced those as well: broken relationships (and the accompanying broken heart), cancer, loss of loved ones, and death of dreams.

It's sometimes helpful to put everything in perspective. Is this truly a hand grenade or is it more in the category of a hangnail?

For instance, ask yourself, would I trade this problem in on a hangnail? How 'bout a headache? Harmonica concert? Hernia? Hair loss? Holdup? Hurricane? Hand grenade? In the grand scheme of life, a new car engine is probably somewhere between harmonica concert and hernia. But I would have traded some hand grenade shrapnel for the restoration of a broken relationship or miraculous resurrection of a loved one. Mostly, though, my problems are somewhere between a really bad hangnail and a mild headache. I've had very few "hand grenades" in the carryon of my life.

We can look at each lemon of life as a hand grenade that threatens to destroy us or as fruitful experiences that prompt us to grow emotionally, spiritually, and mentally (I'll never forget to change oil again).

So that's what this book is all about. Reminding you to always change your vehicle's oil every three thousand miles. In addition, I trust that you'll find this book helpful as you deal with the lemons in your own life.

And while I'll use a lot of humor to make the reading as painless as possible (think of it as laughing gas), I certainly don't want to make light of your problems. I write this book with my own lemon-juice-in-the-eye awareness of how incredibly painful and disillusioning life can be. As I type this very line, I just found out that a good friend died of brain cancer and I've been diagnosed with prostate cancer. (Guys don't cry, but occasionally our head gaskets leak. And I just *blew* a head gasket!)

As Conrad Hyers writes, "Humor is not the opposite of seriousness. Humor is the opposite of despair." I like that! The apostle Paul writes in 2 Corinthians 4, ". . . we are not in despair." And in Romans 8, he reminds first century Christians that "In *all* things, God works for the good of those who love him, who have been called according to his purpose." That's the ultimate punch line!

And so, we'll explore how to practically apply that principle to the lemons in our life and take a look at what exactly is the "purpose" for all these things—even the lemons that continue to leave a sour taste in our mouth and a sting in our eyes.

So, thanks for "squeezing" me and this book into your busy schedule! You could be playing electronic Solitaire, surfing the 'net, or trying to figure out the plot of TV's "Lost" instead of reading this, so I feel honored. And, since the chapter numbers are reversed in this book, you can already feel great accomplishment in that you've already completed Chapter 10!

Keep in mind, it's a work in progress. I haven't perfected each and every chapter in this book. Life has left me beaten, bruised, and bloody (more gory details to follow). There have even been moments when I wondered, *Has God gone on vacation and left a stark-raving lunatic in charge of the universe?*

But through it all, I think I've developed just a bit mentally, emotionally and even spiritually. Just last week an editor emailed me to thank me for my "tireless patience" working with her on a project. I had to check the salutation just to be sure she was referring to me. Maybe those life-puckering problems are, indeed, making a sweeter person. I hope so!

Some things to think about

Make a list of the problems you're currently facing.

Put them in perspective by labeling them with what you would be willing to exchange them for. Would you endure a hangnail or a hand grenade to make the problem go away?

Are you treating any "hangnail" problem as if they were "hand grenade" problems?

9

When life gives you lemons
check the delivery slip
Determine if it's *your* problem

We had just moved into our very first house when a burly police officer appeared at our front door. "I have a warrant for the arrest of . . . ."

Oh no, I thought, *they found out that I ripped off that tag from under the new sofa reads, "Do not remove under penalty of law."* Fortunately my name wasn't on the warrant!

Unfortunately, we learned that the house we just purchased in a nice suburb used to be the neighborhood crack house. And that funny weed growing within the shrub was indeed "weed." What a relief to tell the officer, "I'm sorry, you've got the wrong person."

And sometimes the lemon delivery driver comes to our front door, and our name is not on the delivery slip, either. Fred Smith, the president and founder of FedEx delivery, reminds us that we need to learn to distinguish problems from "facts of life." If I can do something about it, it's my problem. If I can't do anything about it, it's simply a fact of life.

For instance, I can't do a lot about global terrorism. Yes, I can be extra "vigilant" (whatever that means) when the threat level goes from Yellow (Mild Paranoia) to Orange (Moderate Panic). I can pray for peace as Jesus commanded. But, for the most part, it's not my problem.

The same goes for global warming. I can't seal up the holes in the ozone, stop the polar ice caps from melting, or reduce greenhouse gases. I can reduce, reuse, recycle, and buy a fuel efficient vehicle, but again, for the most part, it's not my problem.

Right now another sex scandal has rocked Washington D.C. Problem or fact of life? If my legislator was involved in the actual act or in the alleged cover up, it's my problem since I can vote the bum out this November. But legislators from Indiana have—so far—not been indicted for any kind of wrongdoing, so it's not my problem.

It gets trickier when it filters down to churches, local social groups, and families. What problems in relationships, administration, or physical concerns can I do something about?

If your spouse is an alcoholic, the actual addiction is not your problem. And even if he or she may accuse you of driving him or her to drink, it's first and foremost his or her responsibility. (Don't let them become a travel agent for guilt trips!) It becomes a problem if you are ignoring the obvious problems, covering for them to employers, or in other ways enabling them. You can encourage them to get help, organize an intervention meeting, leave them passed out on the front lawn all night, or attend a support group for spouses of alcoholics. It's *both* a fact of life *and* a problem.

If a child turns into a prodigal son or daughter, there's little a parent can do but pray and stand by the gate, gazing through the tears, watching for their return. The story of Mr. and Mrs. Manoh provides some amount of encouragement. They were model parents. Living in a land that "did evil in the eyes of the Lord," they ate a kosher diet, prayed to the one true God, offered sacrifices, didn't drink, and if there would have been radios at the time, would have been faithfully tuned in to "Focus on the Family." The child "grew and the Lord blessed him, and the Spirit of the Lord began to stir him." Any Jewish mother would be proud to have him as a son or son-in-law. But what was that child's name? Samson! (This is the kind of thing that keeps parents of young children and teenagers awake at night!)

Godly parents can "train up a child in the way he should go," but there's that finicky "freewill" thing that God has hardwired into every human. Even God the Father had trouble with His first two kids, whom He gave His undivided attention. "Look, you two, you can eat anything you want—anything—except from this one tree. You understand that, right? Eat anything you want, *except* from that *one* tree." You know the rest of the story!

More and more non-smokers are coming down with lung cancer. Problem or fact of life? They didn't smoke, didn't live with a smoker, and sat in the "non-smoking" sections of restaurants, so it's not their fault. They can cooperate with their medical care provider in treatment, so like many problems, it's both a fact of life *and* a problem.

As I write this, the world economy has virtually collapsed. The stock market is sliding down a ski slope. Unemployment is reaching double-digits. Homes are being foreclosed. Problem or fact of life?

Trying to sort out what part of the situation is a fact of life and which part is a problem is a tough question, but one that must be asked. We can't take on problems that are *not* our problems. Yes, we can pray. Yes, we can seek help. But we don't need to take responsibility for things that we had no control over.

So, when the lemon delivery driver comes to your door, ask to see the delivery slip. And if your name's not on it, don't sign for it!

Some things to think about

Make a list of perceived "problems." How much of the problem am I actually responsible for?

Sort out those perceived problems into two lists: problems and facts of life.

Make a list of ways to deal with those things that are actually *your* problems. Pray about them. Plan ways to deal with them.

Turn the facts of life over to God through prayer, and then, kick them off your he doorstep!

8

When life gives you lemons sell them on eBay
Profit from the problem

Okay, you've determined that the delivery slip for that load of lemons really does have *your* name on it. Rats! But as the worn-out proverb goes, when life gives you lemons, sell them on eBay!

For instance, in 1834, a businessman was thrown in jail for not paying his debts. He had spent his savings trying to improve the durability of rubber and, even in prison, continued experimenting with numerous additives. Several years after his release, he tried mixing sulfur with rubber, but accidentally spilled the mixture on top of a hot stove. As he cleaned up the mess, he discovered that heating the mixture was the key. So, in 1844, vulcanized rubber was patented by Charles Goodyear.

In 1886 Dr. John S. Pemberton created a "brain tonic" to cure headaches and hangovers. Unfortunately, the Atlanta pharmacist's concoction of cocaine, cocoa leaves, kola nuts, and fruit syrup didn't sell well. According to tradition, Dr. Pemberton discovered some stock boys had added club soda to the brain tonic for a refreshing—and apparently, recreational—drink. However, Asa D. Chandler is credited with carbonating Pemberton's unsuccessful elixir in 1892 to create what is now known as CocaCola, which incidentally no longer contains cocaine.

In 1894, one of the doctors at the Battle Creek Sanitarium, a hospital and health spa, worked to improve the vegetarian diet of his patients. He wanted a digestible bread substitute using boiled wheat rolled into flat sheets. One day the good doctor accidentally left a pot of boiled wheat standing until it became dry and stale. He tried rolling it only to discover that each grain of wheat became an individual thin flake. The doctor baked the flakes, which quickly became a hit with the patients. Later he discovered that grains of corn worked even better and so Dr. Will Keith Kellogg invented, you guessed it, Corn Flakes.

During World War II, British scientists discovered that short-wave radar could detect enemy aircraft, but were unable to perfect the magnetron tube that produced the short waves. In 1945, Raytheon employee Percy Spencer noticed that the candy bar in his pocket had melted as he stood in front of the switched-on magnetron tube. Rather than complain about a ruined lab coat, Spence was intrigued and placed a raw egg in front of the tube. Since the yolk and white of the egg quickly reached the boiling point, Spencer not only had a melted candy bar in his pocket, but now egg on his face. He accidentally created the microwave oven.

In 1968 Dr. Spence Silver, a research scientist, searched for new ways to improve the adhesive that 3M used for its many kinds of tape, including Scotch Tape. By accident, he discovered an adhesive that formed itself into tiny spheres the diameter of a paper fiber. Because they made only partial contact, they didn't stick very strongly when coated onto tape backings. The company dubbed it a failure.

Five years later, Art Fry, a new-product development researcher, heard Silver talking about his adhesive. Fry had always been frustrated with scrap paper bookmarks that kept falling out of his church choir hymnal and realized that Silver's adhesive could make a wonderfully reliable bookmark. Soon 3M was producing paper tapes and labels which became known as the ubiquitous Post-it Notes.

And it's not just products that can be serendipitously transformed from failure to success.

In 1980 I had a dream job—working in my denomination's youth department with some of the smartest and funniest people I have ever known. I looked forward to going to work each day to edit a teen magazine called *Wind.* Six months into the job, the general board cut the department's budget in half and half of us lost our jobs.

The night of the announcement, my wife and I had planned to go out to dinner and a concert I called Lois and told her about the devastating news, but also said, "Let's still go out to dinner and the concert to celebrate." "Celebrate?" she gasped. With all the spiritual and mental strength I could muster, I answered, "This looks absolutely horrible, but I've got to believe that someday, we'll look back on this as a great career move." So with grim determination, we went out to "celebrate."

It did turn out to be a great career move. I started freelancing for other departments at the denominational headquarters—which had also lost staff—and found that I was actually making more money, could set my own hours, and take more speaking engagements since I didn't have a "real" job tying me down. I'm glad we chose to celebrate that night.

But there are far worse things than losing a job. My friend Heather Gemmen suffered through what is arguably the worst thing that can happen to a woman. At home, with her two small children sleeping in the next room, she was brutally raped by a knife-wielding stranger. She spent the next year being tested for possible AIDS. And seemingly worse, discovered she was carrying her attacker's child.

But through the pregnancy, the "all clear" on her AIDS tests, her husband leaving her, and raising the girl, Heather has been instrumental in bringing hope to other rape survivors. Her honest, yet hopeful book, *Startling Beauty,* offers comfort to million of women on national talk and news shows.

Heather writes, "Don't let your pain be for nothing. . . . Ask God to bless you in your struggles, to let you grow from them."

So, we need to ask ourselves, how can I profit from this truckload of lemons on my front porch?

It's probably not financial gain, although Dr. Pemberton's failed brain tonic has sold quite well as a soft drink. More likely, it will be the kind of personal growth that the apostle Paul describes. (And keep in mind, he was beaten up and thrown in jail on a fairly regular basis.)

> . . . we also rejoice in our sufferings, because we
> know that suffering produces perseverance;
> perseverance, character; and character, hope.

I'm still up to my neck in lemons, but I believe I'm seeing perseverance, character, and hope emerging from the fruit market of my life. And, because of these life-puckering problems, I've produced the book you're holding.

So, as we journey through this book, I trust that you will sense there is hope in your situation. When life gives you lemons, sell them on eBay!

Some things to think about

What lemon(s) am I facing?

Is there a possible benefit that can grow out of this situation? Spend some time seriously exploring the possibilities.

How can hope help me persevere through this situation?

What produces that hope?

How much can I get for this lemon on eBay?

7

When life gives you lemons paint smiley faces on them
Laugh at the problem

There are times in our lives when the lemon truck backs right up to (or through) our well-kept and tastefully-decorated front door and dumps a whole load of life-puckering problems on our just-waxed hardwood floor. It's not a good thing!

For instance, in just one week in 1989 . . .

My son and daughter decided to create a new Olympic event—the human shot put. The winners: Faith, 11 at the time, and our doctor along with his stockbroker. The losers: Paul, age 7, with a broken collarbone, our insurance company and, of course, Lois and I stuck with the $500 deductible.

Moments before that, the word processing software went to where all good software goes when an electrical storm knocks out the power.

On Monday, I visited a dental hygienist, who obviously attended the "Marquis de Sade School of Dentistry." Tuesday, we sent our tearful daughter off to her first day of school in this strange new town. And then Thursday, the bank called to say our checking account was overdrawn.

It's hard to laugh when you feel like a deflated whoopee cushion. The writer of Ecclesiastes claims there's a "time to weep and a time to laugh." But sometimes, it's awfully hard for us to tell the difference.

For instance, in junior high (a universal time of comic-tragedy), I tried to ride my unicycle with Kim Williams on my shoulders. We did very well until both of us suddenly wondered,

How do we get off!? The answer? With a lot of pain!

Or the time I visited a young person in the maximum-security section of a psychiatric hospital. I was prohibited from leaving until the supervisor could confirm *I* wasn't a patient. (Can you imagine that?)

Then there was the comedy-drama in the bathroom of a Florida tour bus. It made a sharp right turn and due to a defective lock, one of Newton's law of motion, and several of Murphy's laws—the bathroom door flew open. I wasn't about to stand up and create an *additional* sight on the tour, so I stayed seated until the next left turn when the door closed and I could securely lock it.

One secret to avoid being locked up in the maximum-security section of a psychiatric hospital is to laugh at ourselves. And once we've learned to do that, we've plenty to laugh about and profit from. (Each of the incidents in this chapter has found its way into a newspaper humor column I wrote for fifteen years.)

So, when life gives you lemons, paint happy faces on them. To quote domestic diva Martha Stewart, who has had her share of legal lemons, "It's a good thing."

Here are some suggestions for transforming life-puckering situations into laugh-provoking stories for your next family reunion.

Don't take your situation too seriously

For example, I don't believe in paying a repairperson $50 per hour when I can fix it myself. What do I have to lose? It's already broken, so I really can't do too much more damage, right?

Such was the case with the "simple"—watch out for that word—task of removing the bathroom stool so the tile crew could install new floor covering. And I'd save $50 by doing it myself!

First, I managed to break the main shut off valve to the house. *No problem*, I told myself. *I'll just call the water department to come out and shut off the water for an hour or two.* But then the thirty-year-old bolts magically transformed into little piles of rust when I tried to remove them from the base of the stool.

No problem. I'll just drill them out and run quarter-inch bolts straight through the bathroom floor. This would have worked fine if there had *been* a bathroom floor. A slow leak under the stool had reduced the sub-flooring to the consistency of wet cardboard.

Faith and Paul seemed to find much about my plumbing predicament to laugh about. "Tim Taylor didn't mess up his bathroom this badly, Dad!" my eight- and twelve-years roared. So we gathered 'round the *throne* for prayer and a good laugh.

Some situations *are* serious such as the time Lois and I flew into a remote Native village with an Alaskan bush pilot. During the take-off he casually remarked, "We're about fifty pounds over take-off weight, but I *think* we can clear the trees at the end of the runway." (We obviously did or someone else's name would be on the cover of this book.)

Greek theater divided plays into two categories: "tragedies" and "comedies." Tragic tales had dire endings—such as the bountiful body counts at the end of many of Shakespeare's play. In comedies, however, the hero and heroine always lived "happily ever-after" or at least had a pulse at the curtain call.

As I mentioned earlier, humor is not the opposite of seriousness. Humor is the opposite of despair. It is God's providential control of this world that keeps us from despair. Perhaps that is why Flannery O'Connor writes Christianity is serious business that creates serious comedy. "Only if we are secure in our beliefs can we see the comical side of the universe."

So, the apostle Paul provides the ultimate punch line in his letter to first century Christians: "And we know that in all things God works for the good of those who love him, who have been called according to his purpose" (Romans 8:28).

It's the ultimate "good news/bad news" joke of life.

For instance, the bad news: my wife nearly died giving birth to our firstborn, and we had few maternity benefits with our insurance; the good news: all the hospital bills were paid since it became a "major medical" event.

The bad news: the post office lost my airline tickets; the good news: due to a price war, the replacement tickets were $150 cheaper.

The bad news: I've had some extremely lean years in my so-called writing and speaking career; the good news: through those times, I have drawn much closer to God—and gained lots of anecdotes for books and articles.

And that is the real "punch line" in this comedy of errors. God is able to take tragedy and turn it into a "comedy" in the Greek sense of the word.

So, we can learn to see the lighter side of most situations—or at least be consoled that someday they will make great stories—or an anecdote for a book (nothing terrible happens to authors, just terrific anecdotes). So, don't take your situation too seriously. And . . .

Don't take your senses too seriously

How we *look* at things determines our attitudes and actions. Some people simply refuse to see the humor in situations. Their lives are filled with a dark seriousness. Humor lets us see beyond sight, hearing, touch, taste, and smell to detect all the interesting surprises, inconsistencies, and contradictions to which many people are blind and deaf.

For instance, while in a desperate struggle with an "easy to install"—watch out for that phrase, too—shelving unit, I asked my then five-year-old son for a yardstick. Five minutes—and one migraine later—Paul arrived lugging half a tree!

"What are you doing, Paul? I need a yardstick!"

He looked at me innocently and replied, "But, Dad, it's the biggest stick in the whole yard."

After several minutes of laughing and hugging, my headache was gone, and I was able to conquer the shelves with new enthusiasm.

According to William Frye at Stanford University, laughter actually causes our bodies to produce endorphins that are natural stimulants and pain killers which benefit circulation, respiration, the central nervous system, and our immune system. Norman Cousins, past editor of *The Saturday Evening Post*, claims to have laughed himself well from a near fatal illness by watching "Candid Camera" reruns.

A large part of humor is looking at things from a slightly different perspective, so be aware of the funny things around you. For instance, Lois recently came home from shopping with toilet paper that claims to be "100 percent recycled." (I don't even want to think about that!)

Don't take yourself too seriously

For six years I worked as an editor at a very refined and dignified publishing house. (Can imagine *me* working in a place like *that*?) During that time I saw the emotional and spiritual damage that occurs when people take themselves too seriously. The incredible amount of time and energy to keep up a "dignified" front and the unbearable pressure to perform perfectly squeezes the life—and humor—right out of a person.

Fortunately, the editorial department seemed to attract what the rest of the building referred to as "the crazies." And with that label came wonderful freedom. If deadline pressure became too great, Patsy my editor would dance through the office blowing soap bubbles. Roxanne released her tension with rubber band wars, by calling out for pizza mid-afternoon, or one morning riding my daughter's Christmas bicycle, which I had hidden in my office, down the hallowed halls of headquarters.

One really stressful afternoon, four of us decorated black plastic garbage bags with poster board eyes and mouths and paraded through the executive floor as those dancing, singing "California Raisins." Most accepted it as perfectly normal behavior from the "crazy editors."

Certainly humor that is hurtful or at the expense of others has no place. But humor and laughter born out of the joy of living is a healing and uplifting gift.

We have no better example than Jesus Christ. Yep, Jesus was actually a first century stand-up comedian!

Hyperbole—intentional exaggeration—was the hip humor in that time. So, Jesus would have had them rolling on the hillsides with his comments about looking for a "speck of sawdust in a brother's eye" while having a "plank" in our own. The audience must have howled when he told the Pharisees they would "strain out a gnat but swallow a camel." Or how 'bout camels squeezing through the "eye of a needle?" Or trying to hide a lamp (an open flame at the time) under a bed (a flat, flammable grass mat).

Jesus told stories that could only happen in cartoons—or, at least, with a great deal of computer technology! ("Thank thee, thank thee. Thou hast been a great audience!")

The famous journalist G. K. Chesterton wrote "I am all in favor of laughing. Laughing has something in it in common with the ancient words of faith and inspiration; it unfreezes pride and unwinds secrecy; it makes men forget themselves in the presence of something greater than themselves."

And when a parishioner scolded Charles Spurgeon for using humor in his sermons, the late, great evangelist answered, "This preacher think it less a crime to cause a momentary laughter than a half hour of profound slumber."

So, why not do something unexpected today? I'm not suggesting anything that involves sharp edges, flammable liquids, high insurance premiums, property damage, or hurt feelings. But someone who takes him- or herself too seriously is waiting for your gift of joyful laughter! So, paint smiley faces on those lemons!

Some things to think about

Is this problem a "comedy" or a true "tragedy"?

Will there be something to laugh about once I've dug myself out from under the lemon pile? (If so, be sure to share it with your family, friends, and colleagues at work.)

6

When life gives you lemons join a citrus support group
Share your problem

I'm always looking for an interesting lead for book chapters. So I facetiously typed "lemon addiction" and "lemon support groups" into the google.com search engine.

I quickly discovered that lemon can be slang for lesbian as well as a code for explicit sexual content in Japanese cartoons. (If you bought this book hoping to see naked cartoon lesbians, please see if you can get your money back.) And since there are numerous sexual addiction support groups, apparently "lemon addiction" is no laughing matter.

Whatever kind of "lemons" we're dealing with—physical, situational, or sexual—there is hope and help. But only if we're willing to admit to trusted friends, "Hi, I'm [insert name here]. I am powerless over lemons and my life has become unmanageable."

I'll admit that I've had to work at becoming transparent and vulnerable. I tend to be one of those people when asked, "How are you?" will say "Fine" even if I've spent all night on the porcelain pew with food poisoning. I could have a week to live and would still answer, "Fine."

At some point, I decided I might as well admit, "Hi, I'm Jim and I'm a mess." In fact, I shared a talk at the church my wife and I once pastored called "I'm a Mess! You're A Mess!" After the *mess-age*, several came up to me and gave me big hugs. One woman in particular clung to me and cried, "I am such a mess, but I have hope now that I know you're a mess, too." Yep, I'm a mess, you're a mess. That's why I assured them we have a *Mess-iah!*

Admitting our "life-puckering problems" is often the first step to healing.

While I served as a youth pastor, at least once a month, a young man would sit in my office and say something like, "I've got this problem, this habit. I mean, it's really embarrassing and I can't talk to anybody about it. And, I shouldn't have even brought it up."

I would say something like, "Does it begin with the letter M?"

Every one of them thought I possessed psychic powers! But when I explained that 98 percent of guys and one-third of all girls struggle with "M," there was always an audible sigh of relief.

The apostle Paul claims, "No temptation has seized you except what is common to man," so we're not alone in our struggles—even if we think we're the only person on earth to deal with this variety of "lemon." That's why the writer of Proverbs encourages us, as well as warns us:

> Without good direction, people lose their way;
> the more wise counsel you follow, the better your
> chances (Prov. 11:14 MSG).

Levels of assistance span everything from a talk over coffee at a friend's house to imprisonment in a psychiatric hospital. Let's work our way up.

Journaling

My friend Cec Murphey quips, "I don't know what I'm thinking and feeling until I write it down."

Journaling also serves as a record of the ups and downs of my life. And, as I wrote earlier, there are often benefits that are unseen at the time, but show up later in my journals. That gives me hope.

However, make sure that the executor of your will has orders to burn them at your death. (I can't be completely honest if I'm afraid my journals will end up being read by friends or relatives—or worse—used as evidence in my sanity hearing.)

Friendship

My wife and I have been through a whole truckload of lemons the past few years (and the delivery truck just keeps bringing more). But we have been so loved and supported by our family and friends:

> I wanted to let you know that I prayed for you a lot today. I love and appreciate both of you. Thank you for being who you are and being obedient to the Lord.
> Love in Christ, Stephanie

> My heart breaks for the whole situation, but I am grateful God is helping you and Lois. It will be interesting to see how He works this out for His glory. Like you have said before, it will be a great book someday.
> Kathy

Even our adult daughter wrote:

> Dad, you and Mom have shown incredible courage and class through this. You're my heroes.

Wow! The writer of Proverbs is right:

> Just as lotions and fragrance give sensual delight, a sweet friendship refreshes the soul (Prov. 27:9 MSG).

Thank God, for lemon-fresh friends! But obviously, we wouldn't have had this kind of love and support if we would have simply answered "fine."

Peer Counselors

Sometimes we need a bit more expertise in dealing with the lemons of life. Many colleges and some houses of worship have trained laypeople to provide helpful counsel.

A good peer counselor treats you as an equal, thus, "peer," but has been trained to help you talk through your options. They will also know what resources are available.

They are skilled in "active listening" (actually paying attention while you talk rather than thinking what they're going to say next) and "reflection" (rephrasing your thoughts to help clarify the issue and asking open-ended questions to help you explore your options).

Small Groups

Small groups based on common interests are often safe places to bring your load of lemons. The writers group I belong to is a safe, confidential group to share the frustrations with editors and rejection slips, as well as personal issues. For instance, I spent ten month researching and writing about death for the book *Death & Beyond.* The group was so supportive in prayer and listening to the issues—and horrifying nightmares—the research raised.

Churches often offer small groups for prayer and Bible study that ideally provide a safe, secure atmosphere to be vulnerable and transparent.

Unfortunately, that is not always the case. I once made the mistake of sharing a personal need and was promptly blasted by one in the group with hell fire and brimstone (and it wasn't even a violation of God's "top ten," just some feelings of doubt). Use the favorite ploy of young people. I always knew that the first question a teen asked me was simply a trial balloon. If I didn't go into cardiac arrest or voice condemnation, but instead offered acceptance and understanding, they felt safe to ask the real question.

Support Groups

People with common challenges often form groups for emotional and educational support such as alcoholism, Alzheimer's disease, cancer, death and grief, mental illnesses, overeating, "lemon addiction," and writing for a living.

I'm currently a member of an online group of humor writers that has kept me going when I wanted to quit writing and become a Wal-Mart greeter. Here's an email exchange with a writer friend just this week:

> Surfed around your website again and saw your depression article. Well, guess what? You can add me to the occupational hazard statistics of writers who are mental health consumers! It's so comforting to know I'm in such good company! I live with bipolar II disorder, and have had severe clinical depressions as part of that roller coaster for much of my life.
>
> [name withheld]

> Hey [name withheld],
>
> About three years ago, at writers' conference, five or six of us started talking about depression. We went around the table, "I'm on Wellbutrin." "I'm on Prozac." "I'm on Zoloft." "I'm on. . . ." Every single one of us was on antidepressants! One was on an anti-psychotic (obviously a fiction writer).
>
> I think it goes back to Henri Nouwen's book *The Wounded Healer*. We can comfort those with the comfort we ourselves have received from the Father (2 Cor. 1:3-4).
>
> So, you're in my prayers, friend! I've been reading the Psalms for my time alone with God and am convinced the psalmists were bi-polar. You go from Psalm 22 "My God, why have you forsaken

me" to Psalm 23 "The Lord is my shepherd, I shall not want." What a roller coaster. So you're in good company.

So, since I've been rejected, published, paid, on anti-depressants, and seen a therapist, I guess I meet all the official requirements for wearing the label: *Writer.* :)

Been there, done that, bought the Prozac. At least writers know how to pray for each other! Isn't it amazing what God does through messed up people called writers? But we need each other to keep us accountable to God, to each other, and to our readers.

Now back to chewing through the leather restraints. Ha!

Jim

Jim, you're hilarious! Thanks for starting my day w/ a good chuckle!

[name withheld]

Many of these groups meet online, which provides anonymity yet support. These groups are especially helpful if you want to remain anonymous in discussing your issues. Online groups are helpful in gathering information and knowing that you are not alone, but they don't provide the personal contact of a real, live support group.

Most of all, you want a group that makes you feel safe and secure to share your feelings without pat answers or condemnation. But you also want a group that lovingly challenges you to confront any issues that are holding you back from completely resolving the problem. Avoid, however, any group that promises a cure or suggests that support groups are a substitute for medical treatment.

Professional counseling

Sometimes the need is beyond what peer counselors and support groups can provide.

When choosing a counselor, try to find someone who has personally dealt with or treated the issue you are facing. You'll also want to be sure the person is fully-trained and certified for the level of care they are offering.

Psychiatrists are medical doctors specializing in diagnosis and treatment of mental and emotional illnesses and are qualified to prescribe medication. They should have a state license and be board eligible or certified by a national accrediting association such as the American Board of Psychiatry and Neurology.

Psychologists are trained to diagnose and provide individual and group therapy. They have an advanced degree from an accredited graduate program in psychology, have two or more years of supervised work experience, and a state license.

Clinical social workers are counselors with a master's degree in social work from an accredited graduate program, a state license, and are often members of the Academy of Certified Social Workers. They are trained to make diagnoses and provide individual and group counseling.

A certified alcohol and drug abuse counselor is state-licensed with specific clinical training in alcohol and drug abuse. They are trained to diagnose and provide individual and group counseling.

Pastoral counselors are ordained ministers with significant training in individual, family, and group counseling.

Do be very careful in selecting a qualified therapist for your need. Our counselor believes "half of all counselors are nuts!" He wouldn't tell Lois and me which half he falls into, but he has been most helpful.

The National Association of Mental Health (www.nmha.org) makes these suggestions:

Spend a few minutes talking with professionals on the phone, ask about their approach to working with patients, their philosophy, whether or not they have a specialty or concentration (some psychologists for instance specialize in family counseling, or child counseling, while others specialize in divorce or coping with the loss of a loved one.) If you feel comfortable talking to the counselor or doctor, the next step is to make an appointment.

On your first visit, the counselor or the doctor will want to get to know you and why you called him or her. The counselor will want to know what you think the problem is, about your life, what you do, where you live, with whom you live. It is also common to be asked about your family and friends. This information helps the professional assess your situation and develop a plan for treatment.

If you don't feel comfortable with the professional after the first, or even several visits, talk about your concerns at your next meeting. Don't be afraid to contact another counselor. Feeling comfortable with the professional you choose is very important to the success of your treatment.

Honesty with the counselor—and most importantly, with yourself—is the key to a successful experience. Anything said in the counseling session is confidential, with generally the exception of any information dealing with imminent physical harm to yourself or others.

Knowing what you want from a counselor will go a long way toward working on the problem you wish to address; although it's probably fair to say that most people going for counseling initially "don't know," or rather, they know, but they just don't know where to start—that's why they seek help. Writing down and prioritizing the things you wish to work on will help focus things, and also shows the counselor that you're serious and motivated about working on the problems. However, a good counselor should ask at the beginning of the session what you'd like to work on, or at the very least should pay attention when you try to tell them your goals.

Psychiatric prison

Hopefully, you find help before reaching this level. If you're willing to admit you have a problem, and seek help at the appropriate level, you're in no danger of ending up on the news or in a psychiatric prison.

Some things to think about

Is there a friend I can talk with who will accept me and not condemn me for honestly sharing my struggles?

Is there an online group or support group where I can find fellowship and encouragement?

If those are not adequate, what other resources are available in my church or community?

Join others being squeezed by the lemons of life at SqueezingGoodOutOfBad@yahoogroups.com—the official group of *Squeezing Good Out of Bad.*

When life gives you lemons use as an all-natural, organic astringent
Grow from the problem

Pop quiz! Take out a clean sheet of paper and a number-2 pencil for this multiple-choice test.

1. Which of these fruits has more vitamin C?
a) Orange
b) Lemon
c) Passion Fruit

2. A single lemon tree can produce how many lemons per year?
a) 100
b) 3,000
c) a number equal to the national bailout for U.S. banks

3. A lemon will yield twice as much juice if you
a) Put it in a 200-degree oven for a few minutes
b) Freeze it before squeezing
c) Run over it with a truck

4. Putting salt on a lemon half . . .
a) Takes away the sour taste
b) Cleans the lime build up off sinks and faucets, shines copper bottom pans
c) Makes great lemon pepper chicken

5. Ancient cultures used lemons to . . .
a) Poison their enemy's water supply
b) Lighten, exfoliate, and tone skin
c) Play croquet

Okay, exchange with your neighbor to grade your papers. B is the answer for all the questions.

Yep, putting salt on a lemon half cleans the lime build up right off sinks and faucets, as well as shining copper bottom pans.

And, ancient Avon ladies were offering, as a monthly special, lemons to lighten, exfoliate, and tone skin. (Guys, I had to look that up. "Exfoliate" is to scrub off dead and dry skin. And "astringent" is a facial cleanser.)

In fact, Patty Moosbrugger has written a book, *Lemon Magic: 200 Beauty and Household Uses for Lemons and Lemon Juice.* The lowly lemon is an amazing little fruit.

And, the lemon of pain in our lives also produces some amazing results.

Now, before we go on, let the record show, I do not like pain. Instead of "No pain, no gain," my philosophy is "No pain, no ow-ies."

And I'd really rather listen to that TV evangelist with the comb-over hair who is always casting out "foul spirits" of asthma, blindness (but obviously not baldness), cancer, diabetes, eczema, and the rest of the anatomical alphabet, than author Henri Nouwen who writes:

> In this crazy world, there's an enormous distinction between good times and bad, between sorrow and joy. But in the eyes of God, they're never separated. Where there is pain, there is healing. Where there is mourning, there is dancing. Where there is poverty, there is the kingdom.

Even the children's classic book, *The Velveteen Rabbit* pokes holes in my "no pain, no ow-ies" idealism:

> "Does [becoming real] hurt?" asked the Rabbit.
> "Sometimes," said the Skin Horse, for he was always truthful. "When you are Real you don't mind being hurt."
> "Does it happen all at once, like being wound up," he asked, "or bit by bit?"
> "It doesn't happen all at once," said the Skin Horse. "You become. It takes a long time. That's why it doesn't happen often to people who break easily, or have sharp edges, or who have to be carefully kept. Generally, by the time you are Real, most of your hair has been loved off, and your eyes drop out and you get loose in your joints and very shabby. But these things don't matter at all, because once you are Real you can't be ugly, except to people who don't understand."
> "I suppose you are real?" said the Rabbit. And then he wished he had not said it, for he thought the Skin Horse might be sensitive. But the Skin Horse only smiled.

Philip Yancey, in his wonderful book *In His Image*, documents the work of leprosy doctor Paul Brandt. The reason for the destruction of flesh and muscle is that the victims feel no pain. So, if a leprosy patient gashes the bottom of his foot while walking barefoot, he won't notice a problem until it is infected to the point of losing his foot.

Pain then, Yancey argues, is a gift from God. Without it, we wouldn't have clue we were sitting on a hot stove or a rat was gnawing on our leg until severe damage had been inflicted.

I received such a "gift" several years ago. As I mentioned briefly in the Introduction, I had just settled into my warm waterbed after a long day, when suddenly it felt as if a semi tractor-trailer with snow chains and a load of rolled steel had parked on my lower back.

As my wife drove me to the hospital, I tried Lamaze breathing as I dug my fingernails into the van's armrests. All the focusing on the hood ornament and the pattern-pant breathing of "Hee, hee, hee, ho" we had learned in childbirth classes were summed up in a limerick I had written after the birth of our first child:

A woman named Lois Elaine,
in Lamaze did faithfully train,
Despite patterned breathing with huffing and heaving,
screamed, "This isn't 'pressure,' it's PAIN!"

During the twenty-minute drive, I probably called out the name of "Jeeeee-sus" more times than any televangelist. I prayed that Jesus would return—right then and there—as I writhed on the cold x-ray table wearing nothing but a sheet and what little remained of my dignity after losing my dinner all over the examining room.

Finally, the ER staff—that must have been on a union-guaranteed break—returned and announced that I had a kidney stone. And every woman I've talked to who has had a baby and a kidney stone would choose forty-eight hours of back labor over a kidney stone.

While tapping away at my IV pump's game-show-type clicker ("I'll take PAIN KILLERS for 1,000 cc, Alex"), I began to appreciate morphine . . . and pain.

My kidney would have failed within a few days if God hadn't put half of our pain and pleasure receptors in our plumbing. Normally, it takes arterial bleeding or a compound fracture to send me to the doctor, but within half an hour, I was out of our warm bed, out into the November cold night, dashing through the snow, and peeing into a paper cup at the ER.

And since I was tethered to an IV pole, I had a lot of time to think and journal about pain. I still don't like it, but like straight lemon juice, it's good for me.

Pain produces perspective

Although I had a deadline for my weekly newspaper column that next day and was finishing up a book (I had almost all the pages colored), those things were suddenly at the bottom of my "to do" list.

It wasn't even important that I was unshaved, un-showered and wearing my grubbiest sweats when I stumbled into the ER. And though I'm the type who always locks the bathroom door— even when no one is home—I checked my modesty at the hospital's front desk.

After three surgeries in three hospitals in two months, doctors were finally able to pry the stubborn stone loose. The experience provided a whole new way of looking at life.

Every morning that I don't wake up in a hospital bed is a great day. Every day I can avoid stitches, IV needles, or dry heaves is terrific. And after having "Delhi Belly" in India (you don't want to know the details, trust me), just living in a country where you can drink the water and breathe the air is wonderful!

Lemons teach us to be grateful for the many things in life we do enjoy. (See Appendix C for top ten things for which you can be thankful right where you are. Even if you're reading this in an Intensive Care Unit or the back seat of a Mumbai taxi.)

Pain produces perseverance

The New Testament reports that the apostle Paul was given the power to heal the sick and raise the dead. Pretty impressive pain relief! But somehow God chose not to heal Paul's "thorn in the flesh." Commentators and speculators suggest he was suffering from malaria, poor vision, an especially powerful libido, or all three. Now if I were Paul, I'd be pretty discouraged. "Here I am working 24/7 healing lepers and paralytics, as well as raising Eutychus from the dead after he dozed off and fell out the window during one of my long-winded sermons—and I can't even get relief for my own pain!"

But Paul wrote: "Not only so, but we also rejoice in our sufferings, because we know that suffering produces perseverance; perseverance, character; and character, hope" (Rom. 5:1-4).

The apostle James, who was eventually stoned for his faith writes:

> Dear brothers and sisters, whenever trouble comes your way, let it be an opportunity for joy. For when your faith is tested, your endurance has a chance to grow. So let it grow, for when your endurance is fully developed, you will be strong in character and ready for anything (James 1:2-4 NLT).

Helen Keller, blind and deaf, became an inspiration to millions of disabled people. Corrie ten Boom sat by her sister's side as she died in a Nazi concentration camp, yet went on to write and speak internationally about forgiveness. Joni Eareckson Tada, paralyzed from the neck down, paints watercolors, hosts a nationwide radio show, and speaks at conferences throughout the world—all from the confines of her motorized wheelchair.

The most positive, loving people I know have histories of great emotional or physical pain and yet they have persevered. As my dad used to remind me, "What doesn't kill you only makes you stronger."

One of the things that keeps me going besides Tylenol (for arthritis in my neck), Lipitor (for the cholesterol level of Jack Sprat's wife), Claritin (for living in the pollen capital of North America), and Cymbalta (for being a freelance writer), is the assurance of Romans 8:28:

> And we know that in all things God works for the good of those who love him, who have been called according to his purpose.

Pain produces purpose

Okay, Mister Smarty Pants Author, you may be thinking. *So what is God's role in pain? Does He cause our pain much*

*like a dentist or personal trainer does to bring a greater good?
Or does He allow tragedies so He can come and pick up the
bloodied pieces and make something good? Or is He simply
vacationing in Cancun and hasn't checked His voice mail
recently?*

I can say with the utmost confidence—and I have a degree in
theology and an ordination certificate—I don't have a clue! I
really don't. I do know, however, that whether God causes,
allows, or simply takes a "hands off" approach to pain, He does
somehow personally, actively, miraculously work it for our good.

I've spent a lot of spiritual perspiration trying to answer the
questions of "why" in my life, but I've come to the conclusion
that's a fruitless effort.

I probably will never understand the reason why my second-
grade Sunday school teacher taught us the ditty "Happiness Is
The Lord" one Sunday and committed suicide the following
Saturday. Or why I was laid off from the perfect job in
publishing. (Maybe so I'd have time to write this book.) And
particularly, why bad things happen to such nice people as you
and me.

But I think God is more than willing to answer "how" we can
use these tragedies to conform us into the people he desires us to
be. (We'll talk more about that in later chapters.)

He has used physical pain to move me past annoyance with
old people's complaints ("Come on, Gramps, stop obsessing
about your colon!), to a real empathy for anyone in pain. Yep,
God even works together for good stubborn kidney stones,
double-hernia surgery, flexible sigmoid exams, and central
serous retinopathy (which simply is a $200-an-hour
ophthalmologist's term for looking at life just a bit differently
than normal people). Now, I even get false labor pains whenever
I visit the maternity ward.

But more than physical pain, God has used emotional pain to
make me a more loving, understanding person. When I started
out in youth work during the Polyester Era, my counseling
philosophy was simply, "Get over it!"

And now that I'm diagnosed with clinical depression, I have much more empathy for people whom I used to think didn't have any willpower or control over their thinking processes. "Just watch Robert Schuller and quit your stinkin' thinkin'!" I might as well tell a diabetic, "You don't need insulin, just a better attitude toward your blood-sugar level!"

I even have a better understanding of how God feels. After an estranged relationship, I found myself crying my eyes out feeling so sorry for God. He didn't have just one person from whom He was estranged, but was heartbroken over five billion broken relationships!

I don't credit (or blame) God for any of this pain or planned obsolescence. (I've noticed my face is sliding off my head and collecting under my chin. And, if it weren't for my belt, my chest would be around my ankles.) But I do praise Him that He has used times of physical, mental, and emotional pain to chip away at my sharp edges. And it has allowed me to provide real comfort for others losing their looks, their jobs, or their health.

And so when life gives us lemons, don't ask *why*, but ask God *how* He can use them to cleanse and exfoliate you of the oily, greasy buildup in your life.

Some things to think about

We'll probably never know the answer to "why?" but, we can know the answer to related questions:

What can I learn from this problem? *How* can it make me a better person?

How can I help others going through the same thing? (A whole chapter on that later.)

4

When life gives you lemons don't shoot the delivery driver
Forgive the problem-maker

"I need to go shoot something," I announced to my wife as I stormed out of the house with a handgun, a shotgun, and two rifles. Lois and I had just received disastrous news delivered to our doorstep.

"You did say *something* not *somebody*?" Lois asked nervously. I showed her the trash bag filled with Diet Coke cans and headed out to the country to work off some powerful emotions. (I love guns, but I've never shot anything with a pulse. Go figure!)

I riddled the cans to shreds with my private arsenal as I worked out my feelings:

Anger. *Blam!*

Betrayal. *Blam!*

Confusion. *Blam!*

Depression. *Blam!*

Embarrassment. *Blam!*

Frustration. *Blam!*

Grief. *Blam!*

All the way through the emotional alphabet.

Zealousy. *Blam!*

But Lois, although heartbroken, was absolutely gracious to those who had hurt us so deeply. Me, I was reloading.

I think Christians have a harder time dealing emotionally with lemons than non-Christians. Non-Christians simply quip, "Lemons happen!" (Well, they say something else, but I want to keep this book G-rated.)

Christians, however, agonize over lemon shipments.

Why didn't God stop the delivery?
He could have had the delivery slip get lost.
He could have given the delivery truck a flat tire.
He could have stopped it with any number of Old Testament acts of poetic justice.
And why did He create lemons in the first place?

In the book of Psalms, the writers deal with the emotional roller coaster we call life (remain seated with your arms and legs inside the car at all times!) Notice the high highs and low lows in just three sequential psalms:

> O LORD, the king rejoices in your strength.
> How great is his joy in the victories you give!
> You have granted him the desire of his heart
> and have not withheld the request of his lips
> (Ps. 21:1-2)

> My God, my God, why have you forsaken me?
> Why are you so far from saving me,
> so far from the words of my groaning? (Ps. 22:1).

> The LORD is my shepherd, I shall not be in want.
> He makes me lie down in green pastures,
> he leads me beside quiet waters,
> he restores my soul.
> He guides me in paths of righteousness
> for his name's sake.
> Even though I walk
> through the valley of the shadow of death,
> I will fear no evil . . . (Ps. 23:1-4a).

Wow! Does anyone else need a neck brace?! When we encounter an avalanche of lemons, it is easy to question God's role (or lack of it).

> Why, O LORD, do you stand far off?
> Why do you hide yourself in times of trouble?
> (Ps. 10:1).

How long, O LORD? Will you forget me forever?
How long will you hide your face from me? (Ps.
13:1).

In my alarm I said,
"I am cut off from your sight!" (Ps. 31:22a).

But as for me, my feet had almost slipped;
I had nearly lost my foothold.
For I envied the arrogant
when I saw the prosperity of the wicked.
They have no struggles;
their bodies are healthy and strong.
They are free from the burdens common to man;
they are not plagued by human ills (Ps. 73:2-5).

Why have you rejected us forever, O God? (Ps.
74:1a).

So, one human reaction to lemon deliveries is to question
God's love and providence: *If He is so loving and powerful,, this
wouldn't happen.* (We'll talk about that later in this chapter.) I'm
sure the Old Testament's Joseph had those kinds of questions
when a whole caravan of lemons was delivered to his tent!

Things started out well for little Joey, however:

Jacob loved Joseph more than any of his other
children because Joseph had been born to him in
his old age. So one day Jacob had a special gift
made for Joseph—a beautiful robe. But his brothers
hated Joseph because their father loved him more
than the rest of them. They couldn't say a kind
word to him.

One night Joseph had a dream, and when he
told his brothers about it, they hated him more than
ever. "Listen to this dream," he said. "We were out
in the field, tying up bundles of grain. Suddenly

my bundle stood up, and your bundles all gathered around and bowed low before mine!"

His brothers responded, "So you think you will be our king, do you? Do you actually think you will reign over us?" And they hated him all the more because of his dreams and the way he talked about them (Gen. 37:3-8).

Send in the lemon traders!

First, Joseph's brothers decided to take this arrogant dreamer down a peg or two. While Joseph was parading through the sheep pasture in his "beautiful robe"—a symbol of royalty and authority—his brothers beat him up, tossed him headfirst into a dry well, and then sold him to some passing Ishmaelite slave traders headed for Egypt.

But it got worse. For eleven years, Joseph worked faithfully as a slave to a wealthy man named Potiphar. The master's wife, the original "desperate housewife," tried to seduce this "a very handsome and well-built young man," but Joseph fled temptation and left his robe behind. (Another robe lost!)

It got even worse. Mrs. P accused him of sexual assault, and Joseph was thrown in prison for two years.

Finally, the Pharaoh learned that Joseph could interpret dreams, so the Egyptian ruler dragged him out of prison and asked him what this dream about seven scrawny, sickly cows eating seven fat healthy cows was all about. God revealed to Joseph that this meant that for seven years Egypt would have bumper crops, but this would be followed by seven years of famine when nothing—not even dandelions—would grow.

Joseph's suggestions were well received by Pharaoh and his officials.

So Pharaoh asked his officials, "Can we find anyone else like this man so obviously filled with the spirit of God?" Then Pharaoh said to Joseph, "Since God has revealed the meaning of the dreams to you, clearly no one else is as intelligent or wise

as you are. You will be in charge of my court, and
all my people will take orders from you. Only I,
sitting on my throne, will have a rank higher than
yours."

Pharaoh said to Joseph, "I hereby put you in
charge of the entire land of Egypt." Then Pharaoh
removed his signet ring from his hand and placed
it on Joseph's finger. He dressed him in fine linen
clothing and hung a gold chain around his neck.
Then he had Joseph ride in the chariot reserved
for his second-in-command. And wherever Joseph
went, the command was shouted, "Kneel down!"
(Gen. 41:37-43).

And who should come looking for food? Yep, Joseph's
brothers! Joseph had some fun with them by framing them for
grand larceny and threatening to have them killed or imprisoned,
but after a couple chapters of Old Testament soap opera . . .

. . . Joseph replied, "Don't be afraid of me. Am
I God, that I can punish you? *You intended to harm
me, but God intended it all for good.* He brought
me to this position so I could save the lives of many
people. No, don't be afraid. I will continue to take
care of you and your children." So he reassured
them by speaking kindly to them (Gen. 50:19-21,
italics mine).

I like that line: "You intended to harm me, but God intended
it all for good. He brought me to this position so I could save the
lives of many people."

The bowing down thing was a minor subplot in the entire
story. Joseph, at seventeen, had only a glimpse of the dream: "My
older brothers—even Mom and Dad—bow down to me. How
cool is that?" But at thirty-seven, he still didn't have a clue just
how big was the dream.

We read in Matthew 1:2, "Abraham was the father of Isaac, Isaac

the father of Jacob, Jacob the father of Judah and his brothers. . . ."
Then fast-forward forty-two generations to verse 16: ". . . and Jacob
the father of Joseph, the husband of Mary, of whom was born Jesus,
who is called Christ."

Stop right there. Do you see that? Without Joseph's dream,
starvation would have wiped out *salvation*! The ancestors of
Christ would have perished, and you and I wouldn't be reading a
Christian book!

You intended to harm me . . .

Joseph's brothers certainly had malicious intentions when
they beat up brother Joey, ripped up his coat of many colors,
threw him headfirst into a dry well, and then sold him into
Egyptian slavery.

Potiphar's wife certainly had lewd and lascivious intentions
when she tried to seduce Joseph. And I doubt if Potiphar himself
felt goodwill toward this slave he had entrusted to care for his
entire household, and then tried to sexually assault his wife.

Let's face it, some people don't have good intentions when
it comes to us either. You may have grown up in an abusive
home. Perhaps you were viciously attacked: physically, sexually,
verbally, or professionally. Some actions are obviously unethical,
illegal, or immoral making the perpetrator's intentions clear.
More often, we're never sure what the intention is—such as
those who hurt Lois and I at the beginning of this chapter. (I can't
assume their intentions, and perhaps they were indeed acting
within God's perfect will.)

. . . but God intended it all for good

It's *not* God's will that anyone should be abused, seduced,
and accused falsely. Let me repeat that: It's *not* God's will that
anyone should be abused, seduced, and accused falsely.

But we often ask, "How could a God of love and compassion
let one of His children experience such sinful actions?" Perhaps
in the same way He let His one and only Son experience such
sinful actions. It is only because He knows there is a much
greater good . . . "the saving of many lives." (It sounds very

familiar to Romans 8:28, doesn't it!)
Genesis 50 continues:

> So they sent this message to Joseph: "Before
> your father died, he instructed us to say to you:
> 'Please forgive your brothers for the great wrong
> they did to you—for their sin in treating you so
> cruelly.' So we, the servants of the God of your
> father, beg you to forgive our sin." When Joseph
> received the message, he broke down and wept
> (Gen. 50:16-17).

Please forgive your brothers for the great wrong they did to you . . .

Joseph had the government's authority to have his rotten, no good so-called brothers enslaved to serve him, imprisoned, or even executed.

While Jacob pleaded with his son to forgive his brothers, Jesus is very clear about forgiving the delivery driver who dumps a load of lemons at our front door:

> "If you forgive those who sin against you, your
> heavenly Father will forgive you. But if you refuse
> to forgive others, your Father will not forgive your
> sins" (Matt. 6:14-15 NLT).

> "And when you stand praying, if you hold
> anything against anyone, forgive him, so that your
> Father in heaven may forgive you your sins" (Mark
> 11:25).

> "But I tell you who hear me: Love your
> enemies, do good to those who hate you, bless
> those who curse you, pray for those who mistreat
> you. If someone strikes you on one cheek, turn to
> him the other also. If someone takes your cloak,
> do not stop him from taking your tunic. Give to
> everyone who asks you, and if anyone takes what

belongs to you, do not demand it back. Do to others as you would have them do to you.

"If you love those who love you, what credit is that to you? Even 'sinners' love those who love them. And if you do good to those who are good to you, what credit is that to you? Even 'sinners' do that. And if you lend to those from whom you expect repayment, what credit is that to you? Even 'sinners' lend to 'sinners,' expecting to be repaid in full. But love your enemies, do good to them, and lend to them without expecting to get anything back. Then your reward will be great, and you will be sons of the Most High, because he is kind to the ungrateful and wicked. Be merciful, just as your Father is merciful.

"Do not judge, and you will not be judged. Do not condemn, and you will not be condemned. Forgive, and you will be forgiven" (Luke 6:27-37).

"If another believer sins, rebuke that person; then if there is repentance, forgive. Even if that person wrongs you seven times a day and each time turns again and asks forgiveness, you must forgive" (Luke 17:3-4 NLT).

My friend Rhonda Rhea sent me the following email when I was grousing that this was a hard chapter to write:

Isn't it just like God to force you to sit down and write a chapter on something you're struggling with? I'll tell you, though, I don't think forgiveness is one of those "check it off your to-do list and it's done" kinds of spiritual duties. It's duty because God so obviously and strongly requires it. But there are some issues of forgiveness that are checked off the list one day, then they're right back on there again the next. God forgives once and for all—check it off—it's done. But I'm not nearly as good at it as He is (can we say "understatement"?). I'm convinced that walking in Christ means being faithful to do it again every time it's back on the list. And growing in Christ means that I sometimes get to go two days before it's on my spiritual to-do list again.

The Greek word used in the Gospels for forgiveness literally means to "let go of." Forgiving is a willful, deliberate "letting go" act, but it's also complicated with feelings. We can forgive, but we can't always forget. We can forgive, but we can't stop feeling the hurt or betrayal. We can forgive, but we can't undo the fallout that may have changed our and others lives.

Let me suggest a few things that I've found helpful.

If we don't forgive those who sin against us, God the Father won't forgive us

That's a pretty straightforward, in your face, "what part of 'forgive' don't you understand" command! So forgive like your spiritual life depended on it. It does!

Choose to believe that God can work good out of this bad situation

I've started to see good coming out of the situation that prompted the hail of lead at the beginning of this chapter. In the first edition, I admit I provided too many details—and way too much bile! My apologies. So, in this edition, "disastrous news" is enough details.

We ended up moving to the same town as our daughter and get to see her and our adorable granddaughters at least once a week. But the best "good" was being able to be with Faith as she and her girls left a marriage that had been irreconcilably damaged by unfaithfulness. If we had been living seventy-five miles away, we wouldn't have been there to drop everything and pack up her things, watch the girls when she met with a lawyer, and provide a safe haven for her to drop by when she was having a bad day. She and her girls have not only survived, but thrived—and we would have missed all that if we had been in the previous situation.

People may have had malicious intentions, "but God intended it good."

Holding a grudge only hurts the grudge-er, not the grudge-ee

Anne Lamott, in *Traveling Mercies,* describes unforgiveness as drinking rat poison hoping to kill the rat. It only kills us!

And, taking aim at the people who had hurt us, rather than aluminum cans, wouldn't have accomplished anything except having me locked up for the rest of my life. There are those who think I could have gotten off with an insanity plea.

Get it out!

Over one hundred rounds of ammo did allow me to vent bottled up emotions in a somewhat constructive means. King David used his pen to work through his emotions and even anger and frustration with God. Talk it out with a trusted friend. Journal. Go target shooting (as long as the target isn't the offender). And once that "rat poison" is purged from *our* systems, we can start looking for the good He has promised to work through this evil.

Something to think about

Do you agree that Christians have a harder time dealing with lemons than those in the world? Why or why not?

Have you discovered some ways to break free of the emotional pain associated with someone abusing or betraying you? If so, please share those ways (you do not need to share the abuse or betrayal, only how you were set free from the pain of it).

Does forgiveness have anything to do with our feelings?

Name a few people in the Bible whom you feel had every right to hold a grudge, yet chose to forgive. (Hint: Start with Jesus.)

Can a person freely forgive without the grace of God working in their life? Why? Why not?

Which Scripture from this chapter spoke to you the most?

Who do you need to forgive so that the healing can truly begin?

3

When life gives you lemons
call in the Master Gardener
Take your problem to a higher level

We've talked about handling a lemon of a problem in a variety of ways. Determining if it is or isn't our problem. Squeezing it into a money-making machine (Coca Cola, Post-It notes, etc.) Laughing at it. Taking it to a citrus support group. And using it as a tool to make us stronger.

But all of these strategies depend on human effort and ingenuity. Sometimes that just isn't enough.

Moses is confronted with a plague of lemons. The Egyptian Pharaoh has finally let Moses' people, the Israelites, go after four hundred years of slavery. Now the great leader of Israel is standing with up to a million refugees between the Red Sea and the approaching Egyptian army ready to mete out revenge for that unpleasant "death of the firstborn son" thing.

So, was this a problem or a fact of life? The situation is completely out of Moses' hands (heavily armed charioteers descending upon poorly armed civilians). But also in his hand is the rod that God has used to deal out those plagues of water to blood, frogs, lice, flies, death of cattle, boils, hail, locusts, darkness and death of first born sons. And, beside, God had appointed Moses leader of this operation, so the lemons were in his lap.

Is there a way to turn this situation into a benefit? Sell life preservers? Charter a cruise? It looks like the only ones who are going to profit from this are the Egyptian embalmers.

Is there something to laugh about here? "Hey, how's everybody tonight? Well, 'shofar,' so good (rim shot). So, how 'bout that Passover meal? Great menu if you have to be on the lamb (rim shot). Tough room. I'm dying like a firstborn in Egypt (rim shot)." Probably not!

Support groups are probably not effective either. "Please go around the circle and introduce yourselves so we can notify your next of kin."

Moses and the Israelites needed help from a higher power.

So, just like Cecil B. DeMille's *The Ten Commandments* movie, the Red Sea parts, the Israelites walk through on dry land, and then, when they're safely through, the sea closes over the Egyptians. Final score Israelites: 1,000,000; Egyptian army: 0!

Sometimes, our problems are way too big for us to handle. We're facing a sea of lemons in front and a thundering army of lemons right behind us. But the problem is no problem for God.

Most people don't turn to God until there's a major crisis: trapped in a foxhole, facing an approaching hurricane, dealing with the horror of a terrorist attack, the stock market tanking, unemployment, etc.

But He has designed us to draw our strength from Him, not on an emergency bailout basis, but in a daily relationship.

Life-puckering problems get our attention—just like that kidney stone got mine.

There's a recurring pattern in the story of the Israelite exodus. Things are going well for the Israelites, and they soon forget that it was God who brought them that good. Suddenly they're attacked by Ammonites, Moabites, Hittites, Parasites, Termites and a host of other –ites. They repent of their apathetic ways, and God rescues them. Then things start going well again, they soon forget that it was God who brought that good. Suddenly they're attacked . . . rinse and repeat!

Unfortunately, that has been the case in my life. It's taken my wife nearly dying at the birth of our daughter, a kidney stone, and books that actually sold negative numbers to get my attention; to make me realize that my purpose in life is not to sell millions of books and speak at large conferences, but to have a relationship with God.

But that doesn't mean that God will always bail us out. Sometimes He *is* a bridge over troubled water, but more often He's a whitewater raft right *through* the rapids.

For instance, Hebrews 11, the "faith chapter" in the New Testament, reports:

> By an act of faith, Israel walked through the Red Sea on dry ground. The Egyptians tried it and drowned. By faith, the Israelites marched around the walls of Jericho for seven days, and the walls fell flat. By an act of faith, Rahab, the Jericho harlot, welcomed the spies and escaped the destruction that came on those who refused to trust God.
>
> I could go on and on, but I've run out of time. There are so many more—Gideon, Barak, Samson, Jephthah, David, Samuel, the prophets. . . . Through acts of faith, they toppled kingdoms, made justice work, took the promises for themselves. They were protected from lions, fires, and sword thrusts, turned disadvantage to advantage, won battles, routed alien armies. Women received their loved ones back from the dead (Heb. 11:29-35a MSG).

Wow! Preachers and TV evangelists love those sections! But—and this is one of the big buts of the Bible—not all stories end with the Red Sea parting or David killing the giant Goliath. Read on.

> There were those who, under torture, refused to give in and go free, preferring something better: resurrection. Others braved abuse and whips, and, yes, chains and dungeons. We have stories of those who were stoned, sawed in two, murdered in cold blood; stories of vagrants wandering the earth in

animal skins, homeless, friendless, powerless— the world didn't deserve them!—making their way as best they could on the cruel edges of the world.

Not one of these people, even though their lives of faith were exemplary, got their hands on what was promised. God had a better plan for us: that their faith and our faith would come together to make one completed whole, their lives of faith not complete apart from ours (Heb. 11:35b-40 MSG).

So, what's the use of praying and trusting God if you're going to get stoned (with real stones), sawed in two, murdered in cold blood, and left homeless? Great questions! Questions I asked all the way through junior high.

People flippantly quote Romans 8:28 as some kind of mantra that turns lemons into lemonade: "All things work together for good."

As a junior higher, that wasn't much comfort. How do acne and braces work together for good? (My face looked like a pepperoni pizza with a zipper.) How did women and children being burned alive by napalm in Vietnam work together for good? What was good about my Sunday school teacher hanging herself? And what was Ray Stevens smoking when he wrote that ditty, "Everything is beautiful in its own way"?

Part of the confusion was the result of not reading the whole verse and the verse that followed:

And we know that in all things God works for the good of those who love him, who have been called according to his purpose . . .

That *purpose* is defined in verse 29:

. . . to be conformed to the likeness of his Son. . . .

I was missing a few important components.

Not all things are beautiful, Ray! Some things are truly ugly and evil in this world.

All things do not work together for good all by themselves. It is God who is able to take the ugly and the evil and somehow, miraculously use it for the good we talked about in Chapter 5.

And there are two important conditions. For good to result from "all things," we must be loving God and living for His purpose.

You're probably thinking, *Wait a minute, Mr. Smarty Pants Author! You're telling me that I'm supposed to be like Jesus? I'm not even half way to being like Mother Teresa!*

Great question! Please consider these propositions from God's Word:

God does promise to take that load of lemons and somehow, miraculously, work some good out of it.

The purpose for all these "things" working for "good" to those who love God is to make us more like His Son, Jesus.

That's humanly impossible!

Humanly impossible, but possible through God's "work." Through a life-giving relationship with Him.

For instance, a friend gave me a white carnation while I was in college. Even though it was from some dearly-departed soul's funeral bouquet, it was a nice thought. It looked a bit out of place, however, amid the clutter of textbooks, notebooks, Post-it notes, electronic components, hamburger wrappers, and dirty socks. But it did add a bit of class to an otherwise disgusting college dorm desk. Okay, not exactly a scene from Martha Stewart's *Living* magazine, but it smelled a whole lot better than the room's fragrant collection of dirty clothes.

"I'm afraid we've lost our patient," my college roommate solemnly announced a few days later. Sure enough, on my desk lay the lifeless remains of a carnation.

Monday the flower had looked great as it posed in a mouthwash bottle filled with water. But by Tuesday it was looking a bit brown around the edges. My roommate had heard that aspirin could revive fleeting flowers, but we were all out. We did have some Vitamin C that the school nurse dispensed for everything from colds to cholera, so we tossed a few tablets in the water.

But by Wednesday the comatose carnation had collapsed over the neck of the bottle. Desperate measures were needed! We administered some "all natural, high potency, multi-complex vitamins with minerals" from the hypochondriac down the hall.

But alas, Thursday the flower had gone to that Big Greenhouse in the sky. The autopsy revealed that cause of death was "separation from source of nourishment." All the artificial life-saving measures could not substitute for roots in fertile soil.

The same is true for us human beings. We're created to be connected to our life-giving source. And all the artificial ingredients and multi-complex vitamins (money, fame, sex, drugs, and rock and roll) can't sustain us.

Jesus speaks of our relationship with God in horticultural terms:

> "I am the vine; you are the branches. If a man
> remains in me and I in him, he will bear much fruit;
> apart from me you can do nothing" (John 15:5).

In order to produce the fruitful life described in the next chapter of this book (love, joy, peace, patience, kindness, goodness, faithfulness, gentleness and self-control), we must be grafted onto Jesus Christ himself.

For instance, if you have fruit trees in your yard, go out and put your ear up against the trunk. Listen carefully to hear the grunting and groaning as the tree labors to force out the fruit. Can you hear it? Of course you can't, and if you can, seek immediate medical attention! As long as a tree is receiving adequate water, nutrients, and sunlight, it will naturally produce fruit. That's what it's designed to do.

But Jesus doesn't stop there. He tells his disciples:

> "I am the true vine, and my Father is the gardener.
> He cuts off every branch in me that bears no fruit,
> while every branch that does bear fruit he prunes so
> that it will be even more fruitful" (John 15:1).

So, what's the process of producing the fruit of love right through self-control? Pruning! Ouch!

In 1991 I planted eleven lilac bushes along the edge of our lawn. I babied them from the time they were the size of toothpicks, propped them up with stakes against the west wind, insulated them with leaves during the winter months, and marinated them in Miracle-Gro plant food. I even named them: Lacy, Larry, Laurie, Leah, Leila, Leroy, Leo, Lloyd, Lois, Lucy, and Lyle.

So, when a professional landscaper in our church suggested that they needed pruning after several years of unrestrained, undisciplined growth, I reluctantly let her have her way with my precious plants. Laura was brutal! She reminded me of "Edward Scissorhands" as leaves and twigs flew in every direction. It was all I could do to keep from wrestling the pruning shears from her gloved fist. "No, not Leah. She's always been fragile, needs tender care, and now you're killing her!"

But miraculously, the lilacs not only survived, but thrived! Especially Leah.

The pain and problems that come into our lives often have the same effect. They cut away the areas of deadness and allow our lives to truly come to life.

My friend Yvonne had a horrible marriage. She described her husband as "an overweight, godless know-it-all who never dressed in style. And those were his good points!" Worst, Edward didn't hide from Yvonne that he had a girlfriend and a child by "the other woman." She writes . . .

My husband's unfaithfulness turned me bitter and self-righteous. It did not matter to me if he lived or died, went to heaven or hell, as long as he was out of my life. I joked that if Edward died before me, there would be a drive-by service. I would throw his ashes on the side of the road and people could drive-by to pay their respects.

But somebody prayed for me, and God began to show me everything that was wrong with me! Not my husband! Me! I saw my bitterness and self-righteousness. I actually began to pray like my life depended on it for Edward and his girlfriend to get right with God as well.

It took a long time, but eventually my husband came to know God, he broke up with his girlfriend—who wrote me an apology—and Edward wanted to renew our wedding vows after 29 years of an awful marriage.

It would have made a great "preacher's story." But then Edward was diagnosed with a fatal heart condition. The doctor told them that Edward had a matter of weeks to live—without any hope of treatment.

And so, in a scene that only an overly-dramatic, totally unrealistic soap opera writer who skipped her anti-psychotics that day could imagine . . .

I put on my wedding dress and, while Edward lay in his hospital bed, we renewed our vows. And this is the unbelievable part—with his ex-girlfriend and child as witnesses.

Jesus had completely, totally, unbelievably changed my attitude toward Edward. And even though I miss him so much, I know that God was taking all of the horrible experiences—not that He caused them—but was using these things to make me a better person.

I'm not sure what was more of a challenge to God: parting the Red Sea or changing the hearts of Yvonne and Edward. God was able to take the bitter lemons of this couple's life and turn them into something sweet and refreshing.

But most of all, God developed Yvonne into the person He had designed her to be: a person filled with the fruit of God Himself. (We'll talk more about that in the next chapter.)

Some things to think about

How do I view God? A gardener who only shows up when my life is blighted? Or the branch from which I gain nourishment and my very life?

How can I have a stronger, deeper relationship with God? What's keeping me from that kind of relationship?

2

When life gives you lemons grow your own orchard
Live a fruitful life despite— or because of—the problem

Okay, nowhere in any Bible translation (or even paraphrase) are lemons mentioned. It does have a lot to say about fruits, nuts, and plants, though. You'll find almonds, anise, apricots, beans, cucumbers, cumin, dates, figs, grapes, hyssop, mint, mustard, olives, onions, and even wormwood. But, alas, no lemons even though they are now a commercial crop in Israel.

Jesus uses the illustration of fruit that we discussed in the previous chapter. Paul picks up on the fruit theme in Galatians 5:

> The fruit of the Spirit is love, joy, peace, patience, kindness, goodness, faithfulness, gentleness and self-control (5:22).

Fruit is an appropriate metaphor since . . .

Fruit grows
Unlike my illustration of lemons that show up unexpectedly on our front porch, this fruit is the result of life-long—and sometimes painfully long—growth.

Fruit grows from its own tree
Jesus notes that "a tree is recognized by its fruit" (Matt. 12:33). You don't get apples from an orange tree, or good fruit from a bad tree. So, the fruit of the Spirit—which grows in one's life—is the natural outgrowth of the nature within. John writes in

his first letter:

> Dear friends, let us love one another, for love comes from God. Everyone who loves has been born of God and knows God. Whoever does not love does not know God, because God is love (4:7-8).

> No one has ever seen God; but if we love one another, God lives in us and his love is made complete in us (4:12).

And, as we noted in the previous chapter . . .

Fruit thrives by pruning and fertilizing
If we allow the Gardener to prune and fertilize us, we can expect the fruit of the Spirit.

Notice that none of these characteristics in 1 Corinthians 13 and Galatians 5 are emotions, but actions and attitudes. We don't have to have warm, fuzzy feelings toward someone to show . . .

Love
In both John and Galatians, it's fruit (singular). One fruit. Some have suggested that the one fruit is love with the eight other actions and attitude being derived from love. (That seems to make sense since Jesus noted that the greatest commandment is to love God and your neighbor as yourself. Paul notes that the "commandments, 'Do not commit adultery,' 'Do not murder,' 'Do not steal,' 'Do not covet,' and whatever other commandment there may be, are summed up in this one rule: 'Love your neighbor as yourself.' Love does no harm to its neighbor. Therefore love is the fulfillment of the law" (Rom. 13:9-10). Paul even includes patience and kindness in his definition of love in 1 Corinthians 13.

> Love is patient, love is kind. It does not envy, it

does not boast, it is not proud. It is not rude, it is not self-seeking, it is not easily angered, it keeps no record of wrongs. Love does not delight in evil but rejoices with the truth. It always protects, always trusts, always hopes, always perseveres (4-7).

Again, notice that Paul doesn't describe emotions but actions and attitudes. *Agape* love is a willful, deliberate, I-choose-to-love-you kind of love. (Other Greek words include *phileo,* friendship love; *storge,* family love; and *eros,* physical love, but Paul chose *agape* in this passage.) If it were a warm, fuzzy emotion, Jesus would be asking the impossible! Yet He commands us to love our neighbors, our enemies, and those who persecute us. We may not even *feel* love toward God when we feel He's not answering our prayers like we wish.

Joy
Joy is *not* happiness. I'm on a crusade to purge the church of sappy choruses with the word "happy" in them. The vilest offender:

Apple red happiness, popcorn cheerfulness,
cinnamon singing inside.
Peppermint energy, gumdrop holidays,
when you give Christ your life.

What a load of fertilizer! There is no way to have happy thoughts when Scripture reads, "Let us fix our eyes on Jesus, the author and perfecter of our faith, who for the joy set before him endured the cross, scorning its shame, and sat down at the right hand of the throne of God" (Heb. 12:2). Read that again. Yep, "joy," "cross," and "shame" in the very same sentence!
The word joy is also used six times in the short book of Philippians. Keep in mind that Paul is writing this from prison—and not today's prison with cable TV, a weight room, laundry service, medical care, and three square meals a day. Prison in

first century Rome was often a hole in the ground with an iron grate over the top. And yet Paul is joyful!

The Greek word is *xara*, which is derived from the word for grace: *xaris*.

Alfred Plummer, in *The Epistles of S. John,* notes that joy is "serene happiness, which is the result of conscious union with God and good men, of conscious possession of eternal life . . . and which raises us above pain and sorrow and remorse."

Happiness is based on circumstances, joy is based on the "conscious possession of eternal life" through grace. It is possible to have that kind of joy through the most life-puckering problems we may encounter. It's the assurance, as Paul writes, that absolutely nothing can separate us from the love of God; not trouble, hardship, persecution, famine, danger, death, demons, nor anything else in all creation (Rom. 8:35, 38-39).

There is *xara* in *xaris*, joy in grace!

Peace

The Greek word *eirene* can be translated a number of ways: "a state of national tranquility, exemption from war; peace between individuals—harmony, concord, security, safety, prosperity; or the tranquil state of a soul assured of its salvation through Christ."

Jesus doesn't seem to be talking about worldwide or even peace between individuals when He teaches:

> "Do not suppose that I have come to bring peace to the earth. I did not come to bring peace, but a sword. For I have come to turn 'a man against his father, a daughter against her mother,' a daughter-in-law against her mother-in-law—a man's enemies will be the members of his own household.'" (Matt. 10:34-36).

> "Peace I leave with you; my peace I give you. I do not give to you as the world gives. Do not let

your hearts be troubled and do not be afraid" (John 14:27).

Jesus, as well as Paul, seems to use the word to mean harmony between God and people: "Therefore, since we have been justified through faith, we have peace with God through our Lord Jesus Christ" (Rom.5:1). That's why he begins each letter wishing his readers, "Grace and peace to you from God our Father and the Lord Jesus Christ."

Like joy, peace is not an emotional fruit of the Spirit. It is harmony between God and His children. Not a groovy, 70s kind of "peace and love," but an assurance that it is well with my soul. That's why I love the old hymn, "It is Well with My Soul" written by Hortio Spafford. He wrote the hymn *after* he had lost his business in the Chicago fire in 1871 and his four daughters in a ship's sinking in the Atlantic. Notice the human turmoil—and yet—the affirming chorus that it is well with his soul:

When peace, like a river, attendeth my way,
When sorrows like sea billows roll;
Whatever my lot, Thou has taught me to say,
It is well, it is well, with my soul.
It is well, with my soul,
It is well, with my soul,
It is well, it is well, with my soul.

Though Satan should buffet, though trials should come,
Let this blessed assurance control,
That Christ has regarded my helpless estate,
And hath shed His own blood for my soul.
It is well, with my soul,
It is well, with my soul,
It is well, it is well, with my soul.

My sin, oh, the bliss of this glorious thought!
My sin, not in part but the whole,

Is nailed to the cross, and I bear it no more,
Praise the Lord, praise the Lord, O my soul!
It is well, with my soul,
It is well, with my soul,
It is well, it is well, with my soul.

And Lord, haste the day when my faith shall be sight,
The clouds be rolled back as a scroll;
The trump shall resound, and the Lord shall descend,
Even so, it is well with my soul.
It is well, with my soul,
It is well, with my soul,
It is well, it is well, with my soul.

Now that's peace!

Patience

Warning! Do *not* pray for patience! James writes:

> Count it all joy when ye fall into divers
> temptations; Knowing this, that the trying of your
> faith worketh patience (James 1:2-3 KJV).

The New International version more accurately translates
makrothumia as "perseverance," but it's the same prickly
principle:

> Consider it pure joy . . . whenever you face trials of
> many kinds, because you know that the testing of
> your faith develops perseverance. Perseverance
> must finish its work so that you may be mature and
> complete, not lacking anything.

The word can be translated numerous ways: patience,
endurance, constancy, steadfastness, perseverance, patience,
forbearance, longsuffering, slowness in avenging wrongs.

Perhaps problems develop patient perseverance because we see over time how God works all for our good. I've tried to apply this to my driving. Einstein's law of relativity has something to do with the speed that traffic lights change relative to how far you have to travel, the speed at which other cars are traveling, and how late you are to church. I keep telling myself, "There's got to be a reason." Perhaps God is sparing me from an accident just down the road. Maybe, as I walk in late to church, I'll meet just the person who needs my encouragement or has a word of encouragement for me.

For example, between years of college, I worked putting raisins in Raisin Bran at Kelloggs in Battle Creek. I needed to get my last check into the Credit Union before I returned to school. They would close in less than half an hour, and I couldn't find my keys. I started fussing and fuming toward myself and God. "Come on, Jesus! You know right where those keys are! Help me find them!" In anger, I kicked a pile of clothes and the keys rolled out my dirty jeans, just as I heard a horrible crash out in front of our house.

We lived next to the Capital Avenue exit off I-94 which, because of budget cuts or engineering incompetence, had a very sharp turn at the end of the exit. Once or twice a week, a car would go sliding off the road. This time it shot right across the road where I would have been—if I had immediately found my keys. I've tried to remember that incident—and thank God for misplaced keys.

Knowing that God is in control of life, has given me some degree of patience even though I wish Sunday drivers would stay off the road on Sundays . . . and work days . . . and. . . .

Kindness

The Greek word *chrestotes* can be translated moral goodness, integrity benignity, or kindness, but my favorite meaning is "stooping down." This is not a wimpy kind of stooping down, but stooping down with *power*. This is illustrated in John 13:

Jesus knew that the Father had put all things under his power, and that he had come from God and was returning to God; so he got up from the meal, took off his outer clothing, and wrapped a towel around his waist. After that, he poured water into a basin and began to wash his disciples' feet, drying them with the towel that was wrapped around him (3-6).

If, like me, you enjoy marking up books, underline "so" and then circle it. Only because Jesus knew who He was—and knew His power—was He able to stoop down and wash the feet of a man who would betray him, a man who would deny him, and ten others who would desert him. It takes power to show kindness, to stoop down.

Knowing that we serve a God who offers us His power, who works all things out for our good, we can show kindness.

Goodness

Agathosune can denote an uprightness of heart and life, goodness, and kindness. On one hand, I like the bumper sticker, "Christians aren't perfect; just forgiven." On the other hand, however, I'm afraid it can be a cop out. God commands us to be holy because He is holy. That also, is a whole other book, but I would suggest *Holiness for Ordinary People* by my friend Keith Drury. Good trees produce good fruit.

Faithfulness

The Greek word *pistis* can be translated as fidelity or faithful character that can be relied upon.

Friedrich Nietzsche was famous to two quotations.

In Christian circles, it is the philosopher's observation from *Beyond Good and Evil.*

The essential thing "in heaven and earth" is . . . that there should be a long obedience in the same direction; there thereby results, and has always resulted in the long run, something which has made life worth living.

Eugene Peterson has written an excellent book based on that quotation: *A Long Obedience in the Same Direction.*

Nietzsche was born to a Lutheran pastor, but that "long obedience" was tested by his father's death in his childhood. He abandoned his initial pursuit of theology and, instead chose philosophy. Nietzsche became increasingly less rational, referring to himself as "the Anti-Christ" and signing letters "the Crucified One." He died of syphilis at a relatively young age in an asylum. In these times of physical and mental illness, he became most famous for another quotation, this in *Gay Science:* "God is dead."

Jesus observes, in his parable of the sower and the seeds, that many do give up their faith during tough times:

> "The one who received the seed that fell on rocky places is the man who hears the word and at once receives it with joy. But since he has no root, he lasts only a short time. When trouble or persecution comes because of the word, he quickly falls away.
>
> "But the one who received the seed that fell on good soil is the man who hears the word and understands it. He produces a crop, yielding a hundred, sixty or thirty times what was sown" (Matt. 13:20-21, 23).

It is that long obedience—that faithfulness—through trouble and persecution, that allows us to go on and produce a godly, fruitful life.

Gentleness

The Greek word *prautes* implies a "mildness of disposition, gentleness of spirit, meekness." But like kindness, it is not a characteristic of weakness, but of power.

A powerless person doesn't display gentleness but acquiescence, passivity, resignation, submission, or subjection. Or he or she may try to compensate for his or her lack of power by becoming a bully.

In first grade, Steve and his toadies ruled the playground with the threat of a black eye or bloody nose. But when Mr. Grimes, the principal, walked onto the playground smiling at the children, Steve became a model elementary student. I never heard the principal raise his voice or saw him raise his fist. He simply, calmly said, "Steve, office." Bullies aren't gentle because they aren't powerful. Jesus is both gentle and powerful.

> He is the image of the invisible God, the firstborn over all creation. For by him all things were created: things in heaven and on earth, visible and invisible, whether thrones or powers or rulers or authorities; all things were created by him and for him. He is before all things, and in him all things hold together. And he is the head of the body, the church; he is the beginning and the firstborn from among the dead, so that in everything he might have the supremacy (Col. 1:15-17).

That's power! Yet Jesus tells His disciples, "Come to me, all you who are weary and burdened, and I will give you rest. Take my yoke upon you and learn from me, for I am gentle and humble in heart, and you will find rest for your souls" (Matt. 11:28-29).

Jesus gives us the power to be gentle.

Self-control

We usually think of "self control" in terms of vices. The Christian college I attended seemed to have as its school motto, "We don't drink or smoke or chew, and we don't date the ones who do." The Greek word used here, *egkrateia,* does imply mastering one's desires and passions, especially sensual appetites.

But as we talk about dealing with the life-puckering problems of life, I'd like to talk about self control in terms of the famous *Star Trek* line, "Steady as she goes." I'm not a fan of the show, but every time I've ever watched it, Captain Kirk is either ordering "Beam me up, Scotty," or "Steady as she goes, Mr. Sulu." No matter if the Starship Enterprise is encountering an asteroid field, escaping a black hole, or being attacked by Klingons, Romulans, and/or Tholians, it's always the same order, "Steady as she goes."

Good advice as we boldly go where we have never gone before.

During those moments when our Starship is being battered, it's tempting to shout, "Beam me up, Scotty" and escape into various vices ("Beam me up, Jim Beam!"). Or just collapse in desperation with Scotty's over-used line, "I've giv'n her all she's got captain, an' I canna give her no more."

But we hear our Captain urging, "Steady as she goes." That does require a lot of faith and self-control, but it is the only way to successfully navigate as problems come at us at the speed of life.

Or, to employ another sci-fi metaphor, we hear the advice to Luke Skywalker as he zeros in on *Star War*'s "Death Star," "Stay on target. Stay on target."

Often the best advice as we fly through on asteroid field of lemons is to simply "stay on target." Someone has wisely warned, "Don't doubt in the dark what you've been told in the light." Stay on target. Avoid any drastic mid-course corrections instituted out of sheer panic. Steady as she goes. And that requires real self-control.

Some things to think about

How is God growing the "fruit of the Spirit" in my life?

What fruit needs some nurturing? Some pruning?

How can I tap the "sap" of God's power to develop that fruit? Bible reading? Prayer? Meditation? Encouragement from other believers?

When life gives you lemons give off a refreshing scent
Live a lemon-fresh life

Type "lemon scented" into the google.com Internet search engine and you'll find over 178,000 sites featuring the phrase!

Of course there are hundreds of lemon-scented furniture polishes, disinfectants, and assorted cleaning products including, and I quote, "lemon-scented vacuum cleaner bags."

Lemon scent is hot in candles and incense promising to "invigorate" and "awaken the spirit."

Feeling hungry? There are recipes for "Lemon-Scented White Cake with Milk Chocolate Frosting," "Pasta with Lemon Scented Vegetables and Goat Cheese," "Lemon-Scented Fish Fillet Cooked In Parchment" and "Lemon Scented Lamb with Spinach Potato Cake and Dried Courgettes," (Huh? Courgettes I learned is simply the humble zucchini.)

Thirsty? Lemon tea is, and again I quote, "a zestful treat, delectable both hot and cold. If you have yet to try gourmet lemon tea, you'll be pleasantly surprised by its superior taste. Indulge your taste buds."

Plus, there are lemon scented bar soap, cough drops, refrigerator deodorizers, and even an "electronic/dance/house/techno band" called "Lemon Scented."

Apparently, everyone loves the fragrance of lemons!

The Apostle Paul writes in 2 Corinthians 2:14-15:

> But thanks be to God, who always leads us in triumphal procession in Christ and through us

spreads everywhere the fragrance of the knowledge
of him. For we are to God the aroma of Christ
among those who are being saved and those who
are perishing.

Do you suppose this fragrance Paul is describing which
invigorates and awakens the spirit is "lemon fresh"? If so, when
life gives you lemons give off the refreshing fragrance of Christ.

Romans 8:28 promises, "And we know that in all things God
works for the good of those who love him, who have been called
according to his purpose." And what is that purpose? The very
next verse—which no one ever quotes—spells it out ". . . to be
conformed to the likeness of his Son."

That in a nutshell—or lemon peel—is the message of this
book. God miraculously takes the lemons that are dumped into
our laps and uses them to produce in us "the likeness of his Son."
And that, in a lemon drop, is the essence of what my stream of
faith refers to as "holiness." We try to make living a holy life
complicated by dividing it up into "initial, entire, progressive,
and entire sanctification" and provide several formulas for
obtaining this "second work of grace."

But I've become convinced—at risk of my ordination
certificate—that a) being conformed to the likeness to Christ is
the essence of holiness and b) that holiness comes through
allowing God to shape us into that likeness through hardships
and heartaches. That's why the "prosperity gospel" produces
such rotten fruit!

And so, I hope I've clearly communicated that by "good,"
I'm not referring to happiness, pleasure, prosperity, a "God loves
you and has a wonderful Porche for your life" healthy and
wealthy kind of good. The Greek word Paul chooses for good,
agathos, can be translated "of a good nature, useful, helpful,
excellent, upright, distinguished, or honorable."

There is also a condition. God works all out for good of those
"who love him, who have been called according to his purpose."

Unfortunately, I spent the majority of my life stopping at

verse 28. I viewed it as a deal with God. "Okay, God, *if* I love You and try to live as best I know how for You, then You're *obligated* to work all out for my good." It became a comforting companion to "all's well that ends well," "if life gives you lemons, make lemonade," "it all comes out in the wash," "when the going gets tough. . . ." and all those other clever clichés on those moronic "motivational" posters.

Second Corinthians 4:8-11 reinforces this concept:

> We are hardpressed on every side, but not crushed; perplexed, but not in despair; persecuted, but not abandoned; struck down, but not destroyed. We always carry around in our body the death of Jesus, so that the life of Jesus may be revealed in our mortal body.

All that hard-pressing (a wine-press term in the Greek), perplexity, persecution, and striking down works together "so that the life of Jesus may be revealed" in our lives.

So, if we will bring our lives and lemons to God, He has promised to produce the lemon-fresh likeness of Jesus Christ.

Philippians 2:1-7 gives a detailed description of that likeness:

> If you have any encouragement from being united with Christ, if any comfort from his love, if any fellowship with the Spirit, if any tenderness and compassion, then make my joy complete by being like-minded, having the same love, being one in spirit and purpose. Do nothing out of selfish ambition or vain conceit, but in humility consider others better than yourselves. Each of you should look not only to your own interests, but also to the interests of others.
>
> Your attitude should be the same as that of Christ Jesus:

Who, being in very nature God,
did not consider equality with God Some things to
be grasped,
    but made himself nothing,
    taking the very nature of a servant,
being made in human likeness.

Those life-puckering problems, if turned over to God's love and direction, can create a fruitful life that gives off the fragrance of Christ.

I enjoyed a great year in 1993. My book *Death & Beyond* had gone into a second printing at Tyndale House Publishers after just one month in stores. Two literary agents were interested in representing this "rising star." A big-time California talent agency was interested in signing me up for a nation-wide speaking tour. A Christian recording artist was talking about recording some of my original music. And the church where I was associate minister was growing with plans for a major building project.

Just one year later, *Sex Is Not a Four-letter Word,* (an earlier book with Tyndale House) was selling negative numbers. I called my editor and asked, "What is this? The Twilight Zone? How can a book sell negative numbers?" It really is possible, I learned, when stores send back more copies than they sell. My two opportunities with literary agents fell through. (A third said, "Until you have a best-seller, we're not interested.") The big-time booking agency had scheduled just *one* speaking engagement. Four music promoters turned down my music. And at the church, attendance had plateaued and offerings were down.

I was a good writer. At the time, I had eleven published books, over a thousand articles in print, four Evangelical Press awards and a *Campus Life* "Book of the Year" plaque on my wall, plus a file full of "fan" letters.

But my Christian life was anything but lemon fresh. It stunk like that lemon with legs Rhonda describes in the foreword! I was a small-time author with a big-time ego. And since I had no book contracts, very few writing assignments, and virtually no speaking engagements, I had a lot of time to spend with God.

For some reason He directed this pragmatic Protestant to the writings of Catholic mystics. God loves to surprise us!

Brother Lawrence's *Practicing the Presence of God* was the proverbial knock on the side of the head: "Our only employment is to love God." What?! It's not to write best-selling books and speak to stadiums full of fans?

Saint John of the Cross, in *Ascent of Mount Carmel,* wrote (and this is a loose paraphrase of a translation), "We grow more in the pits of life than on the pedestals of life." It's not having a five-bedroom mansion in Colorado?

And Thomas a' Kempis provided the final punch to the gut and ego: "Be content as an unknown." But I could be such a wonderful witness on *Oprah*!

To quote Judith Voirst, 1994 was "a terrible, horrible, no good, very bad" year. But Neva Coyle reminds us "God is a refiner, not an arsonist."

Unfortunately that refinement has continued to the present! My latest book series, *The Why Files,* addressing the questions of love, death, and the supernatural, won a "Christian Retailers Choice Award" but Christian retailers haven't sold a choice number of copies—and the series is now out of print. Church attendance and offerings continued down a ski slope until, as I mentioned earlier, we were asked to leave. Toss in two broken feet, a $4,127 engine repair for forgetting to change the oil in our Neon, my wife's fibromyalgia (which is best described as having the flu 24/7), the death of my favorite grandparent, and just last summer cancer! On top of that pile of lemons, I lost a large editing account that I was counting on to pay escalating medical bills. We could send out invitations to a pity party, but a friend's experience puts it in perspective.

Kathy and her family have had their share of lemons. Her husband was self-employed as an architect and contractor when the bottom fell out of the building industry. Suddenly architectural work and construction projects came crashing down in the economic collapse. With five children to feed (two in a private Christian college), they quickly depleted their savings and cashed in their pension fund. Just recently her son-in-law was diagnosed with a cancerous tumor near his heart. Kathy writes . . .

It seems God becomes more and more real to me in the hard times. Even though I know He is with me in the good times. Maybe it's because I become more real and transparent in the trials? We began to meet with a group of our church friends on Monday nights at our office to pray for God's help. Phil and I both surrendered totally to Him and His plan to our lives

My relationship with Christ became much, much more personal. I began to understand how much He loved and cared for me. Even though I felt like I was being punished, I know He was actually refining me. My prayer life became more of a priority as well. Phil and I now pray together as a couple every morning before we get out of bed and every night before we go to sleep. (There are occasions when we miss our prayer time together). I talk to Him all day long. My focus has been more on Him and less on me and my problems. I have forced myself to thank Him for everything and every situation—even when I don't like what is happening. I have discovered that having a thankful spirit is humbling but so, so soothing to my soul. I loved the Lord before the tough times but I love Him even more.

God has done miraculous things in our business and the life of our son-in-law. He has caused His church to gather together to help and support each of us. He has provided funds for medical treatments, tickets for flights to the IU Medical Center, food, prayer support and so much more.

We have seen His people rally to help and we have seen His people praise Him, before there were any answers.

Whether the cancer is gone forever or not, God's presence and help was so real during the entire experience. Whether this upturn in the economy and our business will continue to again prosper is also uncertain. But we praise Him.

What looked like dark, bleak, hopeless situations have become experiences of anticipation, excitement, grace, hope and gratitude. We stand in awe of His "amazing love." My relationship is real and what keeps me going.

My good friend—and best-selling author—Cec Murphey faced an even greater tragedy. Recently, his home burned to the ground killing his son-in-law. He wrote:

This morning I awakened and pondered the why question—one I've pondered many times since the fire in late February. Why? Why?

Why is God so good to me? Why has the Lord given me such great peace during all of this? Why do I feel so loved? Why has God chosen me to write and to teach? Why have so many people reached out to us during this difficult time?

If I ever find a reason, of course, I'll know it's the wrong answer. I can say that I'm more aware of God's grace and presence in my life than I've ever been. During all this time hundreds of individuals reached out to us, affirmed us, cared for us, and expressed their sympathy and love.

I've been amazed. Some of them were people I met five or nine years ago when I taught in Sacramento or Memphis. And I'm grateful for every kind and caring word.

This isn't some attempt to look on the bright side of life: I truly feel this way. Two days after the fire a Bible verse resounded inside my head. "In everything give thanks: for this is the will of God in Christ Jesus concerning you" (1 Thessalonians. 5:18 KJV). So much good has come out of the tragedy and I'm grateful. I still don't understand why God has smiled so brightly on me.

God is able to take the very worst that life can throw at us, and miraculously use it for His purpose: that we may be conformed to the likeness of his Son.

The Apostle Paul writes:

And the Lord—who is the Spirit—makes us more and more like him as we are changed into his glorious image (2 Corinthians 3:18).

And, a whole lot of people who are a whole lot smarter than me, have also discovered this truth:

Watchman Nee, in *The Normal Christian Life*:

God will answer all our questions in one way and one way only—namely, by showing us more of his Son.

Brennan Manning, in *Abba's Child*:

All day and every day we are being reshaped into the image of Christ. Everything that happens to us is designed to this end. . . . as Augustine said, "He is more intimate with us than we are with ourselves."
Nothing is wasted, nothing is missing. There is never a moment that does not carry eternal

significance.

Henri Nouwen, in *Making All Things New*:

> Poverty, pain, struggle, anguish, agony, and even inner darkness may continue to be a part of our experience. They may even be God's way of purifying us. But life is no longer boring, resentful, depressing, or lonely because we have come to know that everything that happens is part of our way to the house of the Father.

Martin Luther King, Jr. wrote:

> Christianity has always insisted that the cross we bear precedes the crown we wear. To be a Christian one must take up his cross, with all its difficulties and agonizing and tension-packed content, and carry it until that very cross leaves its mark upon us and redeems us to that more excellent way which comes only through suffering.

In an interview with Calvin Miller in *The Door*:

> The here and now hell we pass through does indeed conform us into the image of Christ, properly understood. I think our unanswered questions prompt in us a yearning, but usually there aren't any answers. That's why the questions are so horrendous. They show us an insufficiency in ourselves that we only find complete when we finally just surrender to the mysticism of the unanswerable God. We have to learn a level of acceptance that isn't easy for us. Without the here and now hell, we wouldn't search for the answers.

Eugene Peterson paraphrases 2 Corinthians 4:16-18 in *The Message*

> So we're not giving up. How could we! Even though on the outside it often looks like things are falling apart on us, on the inside, where God is making new life, not a day goes by without his unfolding grace. These hard times are small potatoes compared to the coming good times, the lavish celebration prepared for us. There's far more here than meets the eye. The things we see now are here today, gone tomorrow. But the things we can't see now will last forever.

Paul presents four qualities of Christ-likeness

Being Christ-minded, having the same love, being one in spirit and purpose

I have been overwhelmed and humbled by the outpouring of love and prayers of friends and family during Lois and my "dark night of the soul." We couldn't have emotionally and spiritually survived without Christ-like people in our lives.

Buried under a load of lemons tends to break our independent spirits. As I mentioned earlier, being tethered to an IV pole does tend to limit our independence. It causes us to humbly look to others for our basic needs: being pushed around in a wheelchair, having your spouse wash your hair, allowing others to take on church responsibilities that you feel you could do much better, etc. And this past summer, while undergoing radiation treatment, I was totally and completely exhausted, so Lois had to mow the lawn. *Oh, the shame! The humiliation! What are the neighbors thinking?*

And it causes us to reach out for support. (I wrote about that in chapter 6.)

Do nothing out of selfish ambition or vain conceit

One thing that a load of lemons does is crush our pride and self-promoting spirit.

Nothing like books that sell negative numbers to take you down a peg or two! Nothing like losing a client because you have, what my family dubbed, "radiation retardation."

In humility consider others better than yourselves

During my brief time as an award-winning editor (four Evangelical Press Association awards) and successful author (four books in one year), I was asked to speak at some large writers' conferences where I proudly shared my secrets for success. I'm still speaking at conferences where I now humbly—I hope—teach my secrets from failure. And I'm getting a much better response.

Working in Christian publishing for the last thirty years, I've been able to meet some of the top authors and editors in the business. Some are prima donnas who demand huge speaking fees, first class air travel, and luxury accommodations. Others that I have been able to know, such as Francine Rivers, are real servants at heart. They willingly fly coach and accept shamefully small honorariums to do what they can for writers and their readers.

I was shocked when Francine asked if she could run an idea for a book past me. Me, who takes a year to sell the number of books she sells on a bad day? She wants advice from me? I love how this humble woman affirmed me with no regard to rank or status!

Look not only to your own interests, but also to the interests of others, taking the very nature of a servant

On the other hand, while working as editorial director at a Christian publishing house, a missionary found out that one of the top executives was traveling to her city in Africa. She asked if he could bring a box of books with him since she couldn't afford the overseas shipping. He wrote back, "I'm not a delivery boy." Somebody needed a delivery of lemons—and it wasn't the missionary!

Paul writes that "we *know* that in all things God works" everything for the good of becoming more Christ-like. He has the assurance of this, not simply by faith, but by what he actually experienced. We know this because he doesn't use one of his favorite words for know, *ginosko,* which means "to learn to know, come to know, get a knowledge of." He uses *eido* that means to "perceive with the eyes, to perceive by any of the senses." Rather than intellectual assent or theorizing, Paul has personally experienced God's working in his life and others. He doesn't hope. He doesn't believe. He knows God works this way!

Maybe I'm slowly beginning to *know* it! And, as I'm buried with the lemons of life, that "lemon-fresh" fragrance of Christ oozes out from under the pile.

Some things to think about

In what ways have life-puckering problems helped me to become more Christ-like?

Introduction

Since I'm writing this book backward, it's appropriate to end with an Introduction because: a) I'm writing this book backward and b) it's an introduction to a brand new person.

For ten years, I've directed a writers' conference at the Sandy Cove Christian Conference Center on the headwaters of the Chesapeake Bay. One morning, while making sure the stage was ready for the morning session, I found an envelope on the podium addressed to "Jim." The contents shocked me—a "Thank You" card with the following hand-written message inside: "We can see Jesus in you."

I immediately turned the envelope over and checked the address once more. Yes, it was addressed to "Jim" and yes, I was the only Jim on the program. I was stunned!

You see, the closer I feel I'm getting to Jesus, the farther I realize I am from His character. The more I pursue holiness, the more I discover my wretchedness. And the more loving I try to be, the more selfishness and ego-centricity I find growing like mold in the corners of my life's refrigerator.

"We can see Jesus in you." Unbelievable! Especially when I think back to my "successful" years—award-winning author and editor, world-traveling conference speaker, denominational executive, and co-pastor of a growing church—I certainly didn't resemble the Christ I was trying to follow. It has only been during my "failure" years—years between book contracts, estranged relationships, being voted out of a church, and having to borrow from inheritance money to make a living writing and speaking—that I have come to derive my self-identity and self-worth from simply being a loved child of God.

Apparently, one doesn't become more like Jesus by being successful, but by being buried under a ton of lemons! And here's the most shocking discovery. Of all the amazing, baffling, confusing Scriptures, Hebrews 5:8 is the most amazing, baffling, and confusing:

> So even though Jesus was God's Son, he learned obedience from the things he suffered.

What? Read that again. I believe in *one* triune God, so it could be translated, "God learned to obey God . . . through the things he suffered."

Perhaps as Jesus walked through life, was tempted in the desert for forty days, and as he was "despised and rejected by men, a man of sorrows, and familiar with suffering" (Isaiah 53:3), he was being strengthened and trained to face his greatest act of obedience: the excruciating beating, then death on a cross.

Suffering prepared the Son of God to obey God the Father. And so suffering remains one of God's most effective tools to teach his children obedience and a life of holiness.

I have learned is that the only way I can become like the Lord I love is through hardship and heartaches. (And compared to three-fourths of the rest of the world, my "suffering" has been the hangnail variety.) I have learned absolutely nothing from success, but I have learned much from suffering. (But there is, even now, something insidious inside me that selfishly, sinfully wants this book to be the next *Left Behind in the Purpose-Driven Life Shack* and make me incredibly rich and famous. Oh wretched man that I am!)

The teachings in this book go against much of what is being taught on so-called "Christian" television. Jesus didn't teach a "prosperity" gospel but a cross to be taken up daily. And, that, I believe it is the essence of Paul's writing in Romans 8:

> And we know that in all things God works for the good of those who love him, who have been called according to his purpose [which is] to be conformed to the likeness of his Son. . . .

I trust this book has been an "introduction" to a whole new way of thinking, and most important, a whole new person.

When life gives you lemons, be conformed to the image of God's Son.

And, if you were helped by this book:

1. Drop me an email at jim@jameswatkins.com and share your story.

2. Visit www.jameswatkins.com for more helpful, hopeful humor

3. Tell your friends and neighbors (better yet, buy books for all your friends and neighbors)

4. Write a review on amazon.com

5. If you have a blog, say something nice about it and add a link to http://jameswatkins.com/squeezing.htm

6. Use it as a study book for a small group and Sunday school class.

7. And, most of all, put the principles into practice to live a lemon-fresh life.

"Dear friend, I pray that you may enjoy good health and that all may go well with you, even as your soul is getting along well" (3 John 2).

$\mathsf{Ti...}$

A

When life gives you depression, grief, suicidal feelings . . .

Here are some resources from my website for when life gives you . . .

discouragement
www.jameswatkins.com/lighttouch.htm (weekly encouragement)
www.jameswatkins.com/quotes.htm (encouraging quotations)

depression
www.jameswatkins.com/depression.htm

death and grief
www.jameswatkins.com/death.htm

terminal illness
www.jameswatkins.com/death2.htm

suicidal feelings
www.jameswatkins.com/suicide.htm

loneliness
SqueezingGoodOutOfBad@yahoogroups.com
 The official online support group of *Squeezing Good Out of Bad*

questions
www.jameswatkins.com/whyanswers.htm

delayed answers to prayer
www.jameswatkins.com/neverlate.htm

unanswered prayer
www.jameswatkins.com/therest.htm

I would also highly recommend these books that have pulled me out from under the lemon pile:

Michael Card, *A Sacred Sorrow: Reaching Out to God in the Lost Language of Lament* (Colorado Springs, Col, Nav Press, 2005)

Heather Gemmen, *Startling Beauty: My Journey from Rape to Restoration* (Colorado Springs, Col., Life Journey, 2004)

Brennan Manning, *Abba's Child: The Cry of the Heart for Intimate Belonging* (Colorado Springs, Col, Nav Press, 1994)

Henri Nouwen, *The Wounded Healer: Ministry in Contemporary Society* (New York, NY, Image Books, 1979).

Philip Yancey, *Disappointment with God: Three Questions No One Asked Aloud* (Grand Rapids, Mich., Zondervan, 1988)

B

When life gives you the squeeze

Here's one of my favorite columns from *Rev.* magazine, but it aptly applies to any follower of Christ.

Great pastors age like fine wine (except for my denomination where pastors age like fine unfermented grape juice.) These are the men and women who, as St. Paul writes, "comfort those with the comfort they themselves have received from the God of all comfort."

Sure, there are young men and women, still wet behind the clerical collar, who make good pastors, but it's like comparing grape Kool-Aid with a fine Cabernet Franc Bordeaux (my Presbyterian pastor friend's favorite). But to be a sparkling, well-balanced pastor with earthy character and a long, pleasing finish, you've gotta get squeezed in the winepress of life.

I have to admit, fresh out of school with ordination certificate in hand, I was not the best at pastoral care: a heady minister with a strong, bitter aftertaste.

If someone came into the office complaining of depression, I simply told them they weren't praying and reading their Bible enough. "Paul warns us to think on those things that are true, noble, right, pure, lovely, admirable, excellent, praiseworthy, so just think on those things and you'll be fine." Until, I was diagnosed with clinical depression!

And I had little patience with those "senior saints" who seemed to constantly obsess about their arthritis, cholesterol and colon. Until I had four surgeries in three hospitals in less than two months!

Plus, every Mothers and Father's Day, I stressed "Train up a child in the way he should go." Until my wife and I were cast into parental purgatory with one of our children! (Incidentally, that verse ends with "and when he is *old*, he will not depart from it." And often, not until!)

Pastors are trod upon by disgruntled members, power-hungry board members and the enemy himself. Add to that the natural frailties of the flesh, the pressure of raising a family in the public "fishbowl" and the unique temptations of ministry. Pastors get squeezed more than almost any other professional.

And yet, if we allow the God of all comfort to minister to us, we can comfort those in the same discomforts.

So, I made myself a list of things I can now comfort others with, that I had absolutely no experience with fresh out of the classroom. In alphabetical order they are:

Audit by the IRS
Building programs
Cancer
Depression
Eye disease (central sirius retinopathy)
Financial pressures
Gas prices
Harassing phone calls
India teaching ministry ("The Land Without Toilet Paper")
Jury duty
Kidney stone
Living in a girls' dorm for six years (my wife was RD)
Marital strife
Nose hair
Obesity
Parsonage fire caused by my cooking
Quotes taken out of context
Robbery of the parsonage (the burglars must have thought,

There's nothing in here worth fifteen years! and left without taking a single thing)

Slander by an insubordinate subordinate

Traveling twelve hours in a van full of junior-high boys (who had just eaten at Taco Bell)

Unanswered prayer

Visiting a parishioner in the closed section of a mental hospital and then, before leaving, having to prove I wasn't a patient

Worship wars (hymns v. choruses, hymnals v. video, etc.)

X-rated temptations

Youth over-nighters, and

Zoning disputes

Whew! Hopefully, I've aged into a mellow—yet substantial—well-balanced pastor with a full-bodied, comforting style.

Copyright © 2008 James N. Watkins

C

Questions for personal or group study

Jeanette Levellie

Chapter 10: Indentify the problem

1. Do you agree with M. Scott Peck's statement about accepting that life is difficult? Why or why not? Use a Bible verse or two to support your answer.

2. Relate a situation that had the opposite effect of its appearance, either: a) A lemony mess resulted in a sweet outcome, or b) A seemingly innocent experience turned sour.

3. What useful methods have you discovered for putting problems in perspective?

4. What Scriptures have proven helpful in gaining perspective?

5. Discuss the context of Romans 8:28. If possible, look up this passage in several different translations.

6. Read Colossians 1:9-12. How does this passage apply to "sour" situations?

7. All of us need encouragement to see progress in our walk with the Lord. Share with the person on your left some "fruit" you have witnessed in their life since you've known them (limit two minutes, please).

Chapter 9: Determine if it's *your* problem

1. What method does Fred Smith suggest for distinguishing between problems and facts of life?

2. Share a time when you successfully used this method.

3. How does taking on a fact of life as "your problem" rob you of your peace and joy?

4. Does the Lord expect you to solve your own problems? Support your answer with a Scripture.

5. Read I Peter 5:6-7. Share some ways you have found helpful in "casting your cares on the Lord."

Chapter 8: Profit from the problem

1. List some biblical examples of people who benefited from their problems.

2. Have you had some problems in your life that you've been able to profit from?

3. Where do you go in God's Word for encouragement during setbacks?

4. Look up the word "profit" in a dictionary and if possible, a concordance.

5. Read James 1:1-5. What profit can you gain here?

Chapter 7: Laugh at the problem

1. Share a past problem that seemed like a tragedy at the time, but now you laugh at it.

2. How does "being secure in your beliefs help you see the comical side of the universe?"

3. Do you agree that "how we look at things determines our attitudes and actions?" If a person is naturally serious, can they learn to look at situations in a lighter way?

4. How can humor help us overcome despair?

5. What does God think of laughter? List one or two Scriptures that show us how He feels about it.

6. Everyone has a different sense of humor. What kinds of things do you find comical?

Chapter 6: Share your problem

1. What is the difference between "transparency in order to obtain help"and "chronic complaining?"

2. Why is it true that "admitting our life-puckering problems"

is often the first step to healing?

3. How has Proverbs 11:14 proven true in your life?

4. Share about a situation where you would not have benefited from the support of friends if you had answered "fine," when you really weren't fine.

5. Why is it comforting to know others who share your same "lemons?"

6. Name some people in God's Word who had "sour" circumstances.

7. Read 2 Corinthians 1:3-4. How have you experienced this truth, either as a giver or a receiver of comfort?

8. Was Jesus ever depressed? What did He do about it?

Chapter 5: Grow from the problem

1. "Lemons teach us to be grateful." What are some things that the lemons in your life have taught you to appreciate?

2. We cannot usually see how Romans 8:28 is being played out in our current problem. Can you look back and see how it has proven true in the past?

3. Does this give you hope for the present and the future?

4. Do you agree that spending a lot of time asking "why?" is fruitless?

5. What is a better use of your time and energy?

6. Take a minute right now and ask God to use your pain for His and your gain.

7. Pray for someone in this class, that God will bring good from their pain.

Chapter 4: Forgive the problem-maker

1. Do you agree that Christians have a harder time dealing with lemons than those in the world? Why or why not?

2. Have you discovered some ways to break free of the emotional pain associated with someone abusing or betraying you? If so, please share those ways (you do not need to share the abuse or betrayal, only how you were set free from the pain of it).

3. Does forgiveness have anything to do with our feelings?

4. Name a few people in the Bible whom you feel had every right to hold a grudge, yet chose to forgive.

5. Can a person freely forgive without the grace of God working in their life?

6. Which Scripture from this chapter spoke to you the most?

Chapter 3: Take your problem to a higher level

1. Why is it that most people only turn to God in a crisis, when they have exhausted their own resources?

2. Read Proverbs 3:5-6. What one word stands out as an encouragement to go to God for every problem, not just crises? (Hint: starts with an "A")

3. What is our purpose in life?

4. What are the two conditions to Romans 8:28?

5. Read John 15:1-5. Look up the word "abide" in a dictionary. What does this word mean in relation to our fruitfulness as believers?

6. How much can we accomplish apart from Jesus?

Chapter 2: Live a fruitful life

1. What types of attitudes and actions encourage fruit to grow in our lives?

2. If joy is not based on happiness, what is it based on?

3. According to John 14:27, do you and I have a choice to be troubled or not?

4. In what area(s) do you most need to develop your patience fruit?

5. What godly characteristics come to mind when you envision a fellow saint who exhibits the fruit of goodness?

6. In the walk of a believer, who or what is our "target?"

Chapter 1: Live a lemon-fresh life

1. Read 2 Corinthians 4:8-11.
a) What are some ways we "always carry around in our body the death of Jesus?"
b) How is the life of Jesus revealed in us?

2. In the story of Kathy, how did she triumph through her great trials?

3. Which shows more humility, to wash someone else's feet, or to allow them to wash yours?

4. Why does "teaching secrets from failure" get a much better response?

5. What is the result of allowing patience to work fully in you, according to James chapter 1?

6. Do you want this result more than you want to be comfortable in your flesh?

7. Pray for someone you know who is in a worse trial than you.

Introduction

1. From where does our identity come?

2. According to Hebrews 5:8, how did Jesus learn obedience?

3. What were some of the things Jesus suffered?

4. Have you had to suffer any of those same things?

5. Read Psalm 56. What New Testament Scripture reflects vs. 9-11? (hint: It's in the same chapter as the "all things work together for good" verse)

6. What chapter in this book was your favorite, and why?

7. What principle(s) have you taken to heart, that you can pass along to others who are "drowning in lemon juice?"

James N. Watkins

Jim is the award-winning author of fifteen books and over two thousand articles.

He serves as an editor with Wesleyan Publishing House and instructor at Taylor University, as well as popular conference speaker. His most important roles, however, are as child of God, husband, dad, and "papaw."

Read more at: www.jameswatkins.com

XarisCom

XarisCom's mission is "to communicate the gospel of Christ in as creative manner as possible with as many people as possible."

It fulfills its mission through print and online publishing. It has been recognized by the Billy Graham Evangelistic Association and Gospel.com for its creative approach to sharing the gospel. *Creator* magazine describes it products as "humorous and witty . . . edifying the Body and glorifying God in an entertaining way."

Learn how you can support this ministry at www.xariscom.com.

34271451R00064

Made in the USA
San Bernardino, CA
23 May 2016